8.85

# RAYMOND CHANDLER'S UNKNOWN THRILLER

# RAYMOND CHANDLER'S UNKNOWN THRILLER

## THE SCREENPLAY OF PLAYBACK

The Mysterious Press
New York

Book design by Michael Stetson.
Jacket design by John Jinks

Library of Congress Catalogue Number: 85-060075
ISBN: 0-89296-128-7 Trade Edition
ISBN: 0-89296-132-5 Limited Edition

# PREFACE

By 1947, Raymond Chandler's stock as a screenwriter in the Hollywood community was at its career high. The screen adaptations of his novels combined with the commercial success of his screenwriting on *Double Indemnity* (1944, co-written with Billy Wilder) and *The Blue Dahlia* (1946, sole credit) had made his services highly desirable. He had already received an Academy Award nomination for *Indemnity* and was about to receive one for *Dahlia*. In the spring of 1947, William Dozier, Chandler's first story editor at Paramount Pictures and subsequently executive producer at Universal-International Pictures, wanted the currently in-demand screenwriter to work for Universal.

A remarkably unusual deal was made with the studio by Chandler's film agent, H. N. Swanson. In those days of the studio system, screenplays were usually written by teams of writers under term contracts. Chandler, himself, had been a team player during his days at Paramount. Rigid studio control was exercised over all stages of writing. Completed screenplays, and all further rights with the revenue that they might generate, were owned outright by the studio. Even major screenwriters with numerous commercial successes to their credit—those relatively few who could successfully freelance—still wrote under close supervision.

Chandler's contract was groundbreaking at the time. The arrangement called for Universal to buy only the rights to film an original screenplay Chandler would write based on their acceptance of a five-page outline he had written. Payment was to be $4,000.00 per week and Chandler was even guaranteed a percentage of the profits of the finished film should it become successful. With only a minimum of supervision by Joseph Sistrom, who was assigned to be the film's producer, Chandler began writing with the promise to deliver the completed screenplay by August.

Realizing this was his opportunity to create his best original screen work to date, Chandler wrote with the slowness and great care he exhibited in creating his novels. The screenplay completion date required two extensions, causing friction between Chandler and Swanson, who feared that Universal might try to cancel the expensive agreement.

By the time Chandler completed the script early in 1948, Universal was suffering the post-World War II recession that had hit the motion picture industry. This financial situation, combined with high cost location shooting and other production problems now made the project undesirable. *Playback* was cancelled by Universal and Chandler's fee became a corporate tax write-off.

Though the writing of the screenplay was especially stressful, Chandler realized in the end that the work was sound. Years later he would reflect that *Playback* was ". . . one of the best films I wrote. . . ." The writing experience stayed in his memory and he recalled the title as well as other bits and pieces for his final novel published in 1958.

In a very real sense, the screenplay you are about to read has been a lost piece of Raymond Chandler's writing. Only qualified scholars have had access to Chandler's long, 224-page first draft dated September 30, 1947, among the papers in the Raymond Chandler Archive at the University of California at Los Angeles. The archive does not contain Chandler's second and final version and for years it has been considered lost. It was novelist and screenwriter, John Sacret Young, who uncovered the final draft buried in the Universal studio archives. This final draft dated March 24, 1948 is a revelation and is the version printed in this book. The screenplay has been tightened and restructured into a 164-page typescript. Dialogue has been condensed and sharpened. The continuity is greatly improved. For an example of the extensive changes, the opening courtroom scene from the first draft typescript becomes a flashback sequence starting on page 36 of the second version.

*Playback* is, in this writer's opinion, Chandler's finest original screenplay. It documents his mastery of the once totally alien medium of screenwriting. Although unrealized as a film, the screenplay is a pleasure to read and remains a vintage piece of Raymond Chandler's writing.

************

Special thanks are due to James Davis of the Special Collections Department of University of California at Los Angeles Research Library for his assistance. All scholars and admirers of Raymond Chandler's work owe a debt to Helga Greene and Kathrine Sorley Walker who have aided so much research. George E. Diskant, literary agent and friend, was instrumental in clearing away the red tape of Hollywood. Thanks are extended to Universal-MCA for its cooperation. Final thanks to Wayne Warga for his ever watchful eye.

James Pepper

# INTRODUCTION TO *PLAYBACK*

by

*Robert B. Parker*

"I was conceived in Laramie, Wyoming," Raymond Chandler once said, "and if they had asked me I should have preferred to be born there. I always liked high altitudes, and Chicago is not a place where an Anglophile would choose to be born." But Chicago was where Raymond Thornton Chandler was born, on July 23, 1888, the son of an Irish immigrant woman named Florence Thornton who had married a Union Pacific Railroad employee named Maurice Chandler. The marriage was not happy. Maurice Chandler drank frequently and long, and Chandler later referred to him as "an utter swine." Separation was followed by divorce and in 1896, with her seven-year-old son, Florence Chandler moved to England where they lived in a suburb south of London with Chandler's grandmother and aunt.

Transplanted to London from the American midwest, reared fatherless in a matriarchal household, Chandler's experiences during this period must have been crucial, and the class tensions and concern for proprieties of status and religion which he encountered in England and in Ireland when he visited his uncle may account for the continuing ambivalence he manifested about social class in the novels of his adulthood.

In 1900, Chandler's family had moved to Dulwich so that Chandler could attend Dulwich School, a public school of some standing from which a number of graduates each year proceeded to Cambridge and Oxford. He studied math, music, Latin, French, divinity, the history of England, and geography of the British Isles. Of the 28 boys in his form, Chandler finished the fall term second. In the fall he played rugby, in the spring, cricket. As he progressed through Dulwich, Chandler's class standing was persistently high. He studied periodically in programs designed for boys proceeding "to business" rather than university. But he nonetheless read in Latin: Caesar, Livy, Ovid, and the *Aneid*. He read in Greek: Thucydides, Plato, Aristophanes and the Gospel of St. Mark. In French he read de Vigny's *Cinq-Mars*, and in English he read *Henry V*, the *Spectator Papers, Comus* and some essays by Milton, and Roman history including the Second Punic War, and the Macedonian and Syrian Wars. As Frank MacShane has pointed out in his splendid biography (from which I learned much of what I'm saying) Chandler learned all of this in a system which believed literature was useful as a source for moral instruction. That morality was essentially Christian with a dusting of Greek and Roman virtues; and the public school gentleman which such a system produced was, as Chandler's headmaster expressed it, one "capable of understanding that which was good; capable of subordinating the poorer part of his nature to the higher part."

It is a code familiar to generations of people who attended English public schools, and it is in Chandler's work the basis of that motif which has been variously manifested in American literature by Natty Bumpo and Shane and Jay Gatsby and Philip Marlowe. D. H. Lawrence has called the figure in that motif a "saint with a gun." Robert Byrington called him the "gentleman killer."

Of the value of such an education Chandler had no

doubt. "It would seem," he once wrote, "that a classical education might be rather a poor basis for writing novels in a hard boiled vernacular. I happen to think otherwise. A classical education saves you from being fooled by pretentiousness, which is what most current fiction is too full of." Always sensitive to charges in America that mystery stories were not high art, Chandler could find solace in the long view that classical training made possible. "In this country," he wrote, "the mystery writer is looked down upon as sub-literary merely because he is a mystery writer rather than, for instance, a writer of social significance twaddle. To a classicist—even a very rusty one—such an attitude is merely a parvenu insecurity."

One could speculate that Chandler's enthusiasm for the Dulwich education is possible only if it ignores the degree to which the sexual sublimation it required may have exacerbated the atypical situation of his home life. And one probably should so speculate. But not here. Here it is sufficient to say that Chandler left Dulwich in 1905, and went to France and Germany for a year to prepare for the civil service examinations. He lived for a while in Paris studying French (he was seventeen years old when he arrived) and a time in Germany mastering German. He returned to England in 1907, was naturalized a British citizen, passed the civil service exams and went to work for the British Admiralty, as a clerk in Naval Stores. He lasted six months and quit and "holed up in Bloomsbury." He wrote some dreadful poetry (though no more dreadful than that regularly appearing in British journals), was a reporter for the *Daily Express*, got fired, and went to work for the *Westminster Gazette*, a highly respected Liberal evening paper. He wrote book reviews for the *Academy*. He did this until 1912 when, with a clear sense that he had no future in England, and £500 borrowed from his uncle, Chandler departed England on a steamer for New York. He was not yet 24.

* * *

In America Chandler lived first in St. Louis, then in Nebraska (where his aunt and uncle lived), then in California. He worked at various times on an apricot ranch, and in a sporting goods house "stringing tennis racquets for $2.50 a week, 54 hours a week." Later he went to night school, learned accounting, and worked as a bookkeeper at the Los Angeles Creamery.

By 1916, Chandler's mother had come from England to join him and in August of 1917 Chandler joined the Canadian army, went to France, saw action and was wounded, transferred to the Royal Airforce, and came home after the Armistice. He was discharge in Vancouver on February 20, 1919.

After discharge Chandler worked in the American branches of a couple of British banks in San Francisco for awhile. Then he returned to Los Angeles. He fell in love with a married woman, Cissy Pascal. She divorced her husband and, after a four-year interval, married Chandler upon the death of his mother (who had opposed the marriage because Cissy was 18 years older than her son). Chandler was now in the oil business and by the mid-1920s was a vice president making a substantial $1000 a month. In 1932 Chandler was fired for reasons rooted in boozing and womanizing.

In 1933, at age 45, with a wife to support, out of work and living on a stipend of $100 a month which friends had given him, Chandler published "Blackmailers Don't Shoot" in *Black Mask Magazine. Black Mask* was one of a number of weekly magazines printed on cheap pulp paper and devoted to popular fiction (detective, western, science fiction, sports, love). Edited by Cap Shaw, *Black Mask* was the best of the pulps and had already published Hammett; in its pages the hard boiled story was mastered and refined. The pulps lasted into the fifties before succumbing to television, and many of the stories stand up, even today, in their direct, active pungency. For Chandler it provided a place to publish while he learned, and a form in which to refine his prose. He had begun.

The beginning was not an unallayed success. Some of the early Chandler is crude, many of the stories are improbable, but it earned Chandler a living (though not yet much of a living) and he kept at it, publishing in *Black Mask* and *Detective Fiction Weekly* and *Dime Detective* for six years until, in 1939, he combined several earlier stories and rewrote them into his first novel, *The Big Sleep*. *Farewell My Lovely* appeared a year later, and then came *The High Window* (1942), *The Lady in the Lake* (1943). He wrote the screenplay for *Double Indemnity* (with Billy Wilder) in 1944. Other screenplays followed, including *The Blue Dahlia* in 1946. And more novels: *The Little Sister* (1949), *The Long Goodbye* (1954).

On December 12, 1954, Chandler's wife Cissy died and Chandler never recovered. He once referred to the time after she died as his "posthumous life." During that life he published one more novel, and the beginning of another. The novel, *Playback*, had its origins in the screenplay published here, and we shall return to it. The beginning was of something called *The Poodle Springs Story* and was aborted by his death in 1959. The last years were awash in booze and loneliness and self pity and one wonders if perhaps Chandler had gone gratefully at last into that good night.

Although *Playback*, the novel, was published in 1958, the screenplay on which it was based was begun in 1947. As Jim Pepper explains in his preface, the deal to write *Playback* (film) was the best one Chandler ever made. It gave him money and freedom and the prospect of sharing the film's earnings beyond that normally accorded screenwriters (then or now). Chandler wrote two drafts (the second, completed in 1948, printed here), but the film was never made. It's a good screenplay and it would have made a good film, but the reasons that films get made or don't get made are (in my experience) legion. And the goodness or badness of the screenplay is not usually one of the reasons.

It was common for Chandler to "cannibalize" (his word) earlier material and recycle it. His previous novels were remade from earlier fiction, a technique very nicely explained in Philip Durham's *Down These Mean Streets a Man Must Go* (University of North Carolina Press, 1963). So when the screenplay didn't fly, Chandler did what he knew how to do. He made it into a novel.

There were difficulties turning *Playback* (film) into *Playback* (novel) that had not existed in recycling the short stories. The short stories were about Marlowe or proto-Marlowes (John Dalmas, Mallory) and were usually narrated in the first person. The effect that the stories achieved was heightened in the longer, matured, polished novels, but it was derived from the same technique. Crucial to that effect was the presence of a particular kind of man, Marlowe (or Marlowesque predecessors). The man was someone we cared about, believed in, and liked. He was a man sufficiently romantic and sentimental so that we accepted as consistent and compelling the sentimentality and romanticism which mark all of Chandler's work. We accept it, not only because he is capable of such feelings, but because he balances them with a clear-eyed cynical toughness that saves him from foolishness, or makes what foolishness he commits not naiveté but compassion, informed sentimentality if you will.

The trick of this of course is the narrative technique. The stories are told in Marlowe's voice, filtered through Marlowe's perception so that we see not only how mean the streets are, but how compassionately (or romantically, or sentimentally) Marlowe responds to them. The result is to present a whole world: mean, compassionate, sentimental, hard nosed, romantic, vulnerable, loving and tough. A world summed up in the central figure, the hero, Marlowe, who is all of these things. And we believe in him, so we believe in that world, the great wrong place which he inhabits.

But the film was not about Marlowe, and the qualities that Marlowe embodies are spread around among several figures, coalescing most richly in the character of Killaine, the homicide detective. But Killaine is not the hero. He doesn't appear until p. 28. And he doesn't tell the story. There was a problem and Chandler was aware of it. Writing to his agent, H. N. Swanson, in January of 1953, Chandler said of *Playback* (film):

> I think it would make a fairly good story, but the difficulty of adapting it as a novelette with Philip Marlowe as the main character is that so much of the best action takes place outside the ken of the dick. I don't mean that it's impossible, but the results, if achieved, would have very little of the original in it except a few of the characters and a basic situation of a girl who has narrowly escaped taking the rap for a murder she didn't commit, and then going a long way off to try to hide under a different name and suddenly found herself in a situation so similar to the original catastrophe that she doesn't dare give an account of herself, especially as it looked as though the second guy who was murdered was using his knowledge of her identity to blackmail her.

It apparently never occurred to Chandler that he might write a novel which was not about Marlowe, and since it didn't, he had to wrestle his *Playback* story into the Marlowe narrative frame—a frame defined by the sardonic and sentimental first person narrator. Having chosen to do this he is forced to abandon all but the germ of the story and a few of the names. Everything that happens must happen before Marlowe's eyes; gone thus are the flashback scenes of the courtroom, replaced of necessity by a much less forceful recapitulation by Betty's father-in-law. Gone are the interaction between Betty Mayfield and Larry Mitchell, between Clark Brandon and Betty Mayfield. Gone is the relationship between Margo West and Larry Mitchell, except the small parcel suggested by Mr. Clarendon. In a first person narration all of these events, necessarily taking place in private, are no longer available to us, because they are not available to Marlowe.

Each of these relationships enlarged our understanding of what was happening, and increased the density of the screenplay version with a kind of emotional plenitude which the third person narration mode of the screenplay permitted.

The opening sequence aboard the train bound for Vancouver shows us Chandler's mastery of realistic detail. The Olsons, from whom we will never hear again, are given the kind of careful attention that Chandler gave to all his minor characters, an attention that created the rich realistic ambience in which Chandler's often larger than life romances flourished. The small remark about Jack Benny being born in Waukegan, and the puzzlement of the Canadian official establish the border-ness of the scene; while the contented couple, in their ordinariness, heighten the discontent and unusualness of the interplay between Larry Mitchell and Betty Mayfield.

In the screenplay, we learn early in the course of action of Betty's problem as she flashes back to the trial. In the novel we are denied that knowledge until nearly the end. If the novel is about the reiteration of tragedy (and the title would suggest this) we have no way to savour the irony of Betty's situation until we have nearly finished. The irony is kept continuously before us in the screenplay, from the point of flashback, onward.

That such a theme was Chandler's plan for the screenplay is clear by his initial treatment.

> The crucial week in the life of a girl who decides to spend it in a tower suite in a hotel, under an assumed name, her identity thoroughly concealed with great care, to accept what comes, and at the end of the week to jump to her death.

> During this week the frustrations and tragedies of her life are repeated in capsule form, so that it almost appears that she brought her destiny with her, and that wherever she went the same sort of thing would happen to her.

It is a very hard go to articulate this subject in the first person narration of someone who is not the woman who plans to kill herself in a week. But more simply than the technical problems of narrative point of view, Marlowe's appearance in the story makes him the protagonist, not Betty. The novels are always about Marlowe, not about any of the other characters. And while the other characters may be seen vividly and interestingly and sympathetically, they are seen through Marlowe's eyes and are rendered interesting or vivid because of their impact on Marlowe and our opportunity to share his response to that impact.

In short, the problem with the novel was Marlowe's presence. The problem with the movie was Marlowe's absence. The movie's weakness seems to me to be in the lack of an interesting hero. Betty Mayfield is central, but basically the victim. She does not make things happen, they happen to her. Brandon's villainy, and then his final chivalric moment, are not compellingly believable because we don't know him well enough, and we have no Marlovian narrator to interpret him. Killaine should be the hero, but his sporadic appearance, and his very incredible (because very sudden) love for Betty are a problem, as is his vacillation between love and duty (a vacillation which weakens him because it evokes pity more than respect). Had Killaine been Marlowe we would have come to know him and believe his romanticism and his struggle (though not his vacillation). The novel's weakness (and surely it is the weakest of Chandler's seven) is that the story is about Betty Mayfield, and the novel is about Marlowe.

The great strength of the screenplay is in Chandler's dialogue, always pungeant and interesting; and in his affection for the characters. Even the bad people in Chandler's work are not unreedemed or unreedeemable. The worst, like Larry Mitchell, are users and exploiters, but one feels somehow that they are victims of their past. It is a past that has left them scornful of everything including themselves, and the self derision seems to evoke not hatred but pity. The more prominent bad guys (for example Clark Brandon) redeem themselves through gallantry. Even minor characters, contrived largely to swell a progress, are carefully wrought and saved from disdain through a sense of humor, or a touch of courage, or a hard eye for life's reality—like Gobel. The affection for his characters gave Chandler's work a wholeness and credibility that few writers have exceeded and it is manifest in this screenplay as much as in any of the novels.

A screenplay is not a novel and can't be read as such. While that insight probably won't get me a fellowship at film school, it needs to be remembered. What seems incredible in screenplays may very well be convincing in the actual film when enacted by a skilled actor, edited by a clever director and scored with compelling music.

Moreover a screenplay at the stage this one had reached is still far from a movie and is intended much more often to be read as a persuasive device by prospective stars, directors and financiers. All of that being said it remains, I think, fair to complain that a screenplay ought to have a compelling central figure, and to complain equally that a novel ought either to be about the compelling central figure, or take place within his narrative vision.

Chandler's place in literary history does not depend on his screenwriting (think of someone's which does) and, fortunately, does not rest upon *Playback* (novel) either; though one is always pleased to meet Marlowe, even in straitened circumstances. Marlowe is Chandler's triumph, and when he found himself in environs for which he was suited, he earned for his creator a place of permanence in this country's literature with the other great vernacular artists.

Reading the novel and film versions of *Playback* affords us a rare and splendid opportunity to see how precise a fit is needed between hero and milieu. Imagine if we had the chance to read *Huckleberry Finn* in a third person vernacular, without Huck. The chance to encounter weak Chandler allows us to understand better how strong Chandler could be, and, more usefully, to understand how he achieved his strength.

FADE IN

1    LONG SHOT—OPEN LANDSCAPE WITH RAILROAD TRACKS—DAY

A streamliner coming TOWARDS CAMERA which is off to one side of tracks. The landscape has pine and fir trees and is a northern Washington landscape. As the streamliner passes, the CAMERA PANS around following it and stops. The streamliner tears off into the distance and in the foreground is now seen a railroad sign, EVERETT, WASH.

DISSOLVE TO

2    INTERIOR CORRIDOR—STREAMLINER IN MOTION—SHOWING OPEN DOORS OF FOUR ROOMETTES

Through their windows can be seen the landscape through which the train is passing. In the first roomette, counting from the left, is a well-dressed, rather wise-looking female, young, smart. She is making up her face. In the second is a middle-aged couple, a Canadian Immigration Inspector and a Canadian Customs Inspector. In the third, Betty Mayfield is seated near the window, turning over the pages of a magazine. She is about 27 years old, beautiful, blonde, and has a remote troubled expression, as though her thoughts were far away. The fourth is empty. There is a man's suitcase in evidence on the seat. Larry Mitchell enters from the left. He is tall, good-looking, young, with superficial charm and rather too much self-assurance. He glances in at the woman in the first roomette, stops in the door and leans against it. We MOVE IN so that this becomes a SHOT of the single roomette. OVER SCENE is HEARD the voice of the Canadian Immigration Officer.

> CANADIAN OFFICIAL
> *(OVER SCENE)*
> Good afternoon. Your name, please.

> PASSENGER
> *(OVER SCENE)*
> George Olson.

> MITCHELL
> *(to the unknown woman)*
> Better stop while it's still perfect.

She looks up at him with a slow stare.

CANADIAN OFFICIAL
*(OVER SCENE)*
And where were you born, Mr. Olson?

VOICE OF PASSENGER
Waukegan, Illinois.

UNKNOWN WOMAN
*(to Mitchell)*
Is there something I can do for you?

MITCHELL
There are a lot of things you could do for me.

VOICE OF IMMIGRATION INSPECTOR
And this is your wife, Mr. Olson?

VOICE OF PASSENGER
Yes. She was born in Waukegan, too. Same as Jack
Benny, you know.

VOICE OF OFFICER
*(puzzled)*
Jack Benny?

UNKNOWN WOMAN
*(to Mitchell)*
Well, there's something you could do for me.

MITCHELL
I'd be delighted.

UNKNOWN WOMAN
You can move to one side. So my husband can get
in.

Mitchell glances back, then moves to one side with a smile.
He is quite unperturbed. A rather decrepit man creeps past
him into the roomette with the unknown woman. She gives
Mitchell a quick flashing smile. Mitchell grins, turns away.
CAMERA PULLS BACK AND PANS HIM PAST THE NEXT
ROOMETTE. We now see the Immigration and Customs
Officials and the two middle-aged passengers.

CUSTOMS OFFICIAL
*(to Olson)*
Any firearms? Dutiable articles of any kind, Mr.
Olson?

Olson shakes his head. CAMERA PANS Mitchell past this
door to the door of Betty Mayfield's roomette. He leans in this
as he did in the unknown woman's roomette.

MITCHELL
*(to Betty)*
Would you care to see the Seattle paper?

Betty turns slowly, stares at him.

BETTY
No thanks. I've seen Seattle.

MITCHELL
My name's Larry Mitchell. I live at Vancouver.

Betty says nothing.

MITCHELL
Same as an hour ago. Remember? I'm the steady
type.

BETTY
*(coldly)*
I'm afraid there's nothing I can do about it, Mr.
Mitchell.

CAMERA NOW HAS MOVED IN CLOSE ENOUGH TO
EXCLUDE THE OTHER ROOMETTES COMPLETELY.

MITCHELL
You could tell me your name. And where you're
going.

BETTY
How far does this train go?

MITCHELL
Vancouver, B.C.

3

                              BETTY
          I'm going to Vancouver, Mr. Mitchell.

She picks up a magazine and opens it, ignoring him.

                            MITCHELL
          O.K. Be rugged.

He turns, starts out, then looks back at her.

                            MITCHELL
          You're next for the Immigration and Customs. I
          trust your papers are all in order.

Betty looks up quickly and cannot conceal a startled expression. Mitchell reacts. CAMERA PULLS BACK as he comes
out into corridor, looks towards the roomette in which the
officials are, then turns towards the next roomette and goes
into it. Fusses with his suitcase. CAMERA PANS across to the
officials coming out of Olson's roomette. As they come out of
Olson's roomette,

              CANADIAN IMMIGRATION OFFICIAL
          I hope you will enjoy your stay in Canada, Mr.
          Olson.
                         OLSON'S VOICE
                          (OVER SCENE)
          Thanks.
Canadian officials then go on to Betty's roomette, enter.

              CANADIAN IMMIGRATION OFFICIAL
          Your name, please.

                              BETTY
          Betty—Mayfield.

There is a perceptible hesitation which the immigration
official notices.

                            OFFICIAL
          Betty Mayfield. Miss or Mrs.?

Mitchell is seen in his roomette, standing near the door
listening.

                                4

                          BETTY
Miss Mayfield.

                         OFFICIAL
And where were you born, Miss Mayfield?

                          BETTY
New York City.

The official is a little suspicious. He looks down at Betty's
hands which are clasped in her lap.

                         OFFICIAL
I see you are wearing a wedding ring.

                          BETTY
I've been married. My husband—
          *(she breaks off and bites her lip)*

                        INSPECTOR
Then I take it Mayfield was not your married name?

He is very polite, but is building up to asking for some
identification papers. On this cue, Mitchell comes out of his
roomette, crosses, enters Betty's roomette. CAMERA MOVES
IN.

                         MITCHELL
I've wired ahead to—

He breaks off, turns to Inspector, recognizes him.

                         MITCHELL
Inspector Gillette, isn't it? I'm Larry Mitchell.
We've met before, several times.

He takes out wallet and holds it out to Inspector.

                         MITCHELL
I cross the border so often I carry an identification
card.

                        INSPECTOR
          *(glancing at card)*
Yes, I remember you, Mr. Mitchell.
          *(glancing at Betty)*
You know this lady?

                            5

MITCHELL
Very well. Since 1940, at least. I met her—let me
see—it was New York City, wasn't it, Betty?

Betty nods silently. Inspector turns back to her, handing
Mitchell's wallet back.

INSPECTOR
(to Betty)
How long do you expect to be in Canada, Miss
Mayfield?

BETTY
Oh—a month.

INSPECTOR
(making up his mind)
Thank you. I hope you have a pleasant trip.

He turns away, starts out.

CUSTOMS INSPECTOR
(to Betty)
Any firearms? Dutiable articles of any kind?

BETTY
No.

CUSTOMS OFFICIAL
Thank you.

He marks her baggage.

MITCHELL
(to Customs Inspector)
My suitcases are open in the next room.

CUSTOMS INSPECTOR
(to Mitchell)
Anything dutiable, Mr. Mitchell?

MITCHELL
No. Nothing.

CUSTOMS INSPECTOR

Thank you.

Customs Inspector goes out. Mitchell sits down, looks at Betty coolly. She avoids his eyes.

MITCHELL

Better get rid of the wedding ring. That's what threw him.

Betty looks out of the window, says nothing.

MITCHELL

Trouble?

Betty turns her head and looks at him without speaking. Her face is empty of expression.

MITCHELL

Or Reno?
(pause)
They always throw them off the bridge there, I've heard.

BETTY

Perhaps I don't take it so lightly.

MITCHELL

Where are you staying in Vancouver? It's pretty crowded you know.

BETTY

Is it? I expected to go to the Vancouver Royal. Should I have a reservation?

MITCHELL

I'll make one for you.
(pause)
I live there.

BETTY
(doubtfully)

Well—

7

MITCHELL
*(quietly)*
A very small service. It doesn't even ask for thanks. How long for?

BETTY
I really don't know.

MITCHELL
Indefinitely?

BETTY
*(with a shrug)*
I don't know.

MITCHELL
*(eyeing her thoughtfully)*
You don't know.

He turns and goes. She looks after him, puzzled and rather attracted. Then this mood passes and she relapses again into her listless, hopeless manner. She reaches for the magazine and starts to leaf through its pages indifferently, as we

DISSOLVE TO

3   EXTERIOR. VANCOUVER ROYAL HOTEL—LONG SHOT—DAY

It is a massive brick and sandstone building, set in beautiful gardens which slope down towards Puget Sound.

4   CLOSER SHOT—THE ENTRANCE

A taxi drives up, Larry Mitchell and Betty get out, Porter comes forward, takes their luggage, etc. Larry pays taxi and they start in through entrance.

5   INTERIOR. LOBBY—THE DESK

Larry and Betty come up to it, bellhop carrying hand luggage.

HOTEL CLERK
Good afternoon, Mr. Mitchell. Have a nice trip? Glad to see you back.

MITCHELL
Fine, thanks. This is Miss Betty Mayfield. You have
a reservation for her.

CLERK
Miss Mayfield. Yes, indeed. A balcony room on the
top floor. Magnificent view. Nothing above it but
the penthouse.

He pushes registration pad towards Betty, and she signs.
Mitchell turns, looks out across lobby. A malicious smile
moves his lips.

6     WHAT HE SEES

One side of the lobby is a glassed-in terrace. It is tea time and
a couple of large tea wagons are being pushed around among
the guests by footmen in uniform. With each tea wagon are
two neat maids, who set out cups, pass sandwiches, cakes,
etc., while the footman pours the tea.

7     CLOSER SHOT

A tea wagon beside a table at which sit Mr. Clarendon and
Margo West. Mr. Clarendon is elegant, white-haired, aristo-
cratic-looking—a cane and spats type. Margo is handsome,
thirtyish, almost overpoweringly well-dressed. Obviously
money, obviously been around. Margo is studying her face in
a pocket mirror. Tea wagon and maids move away.

MARGO
I'm getting positively haggard. In a couple of years
people will be describing me as well-preserved.

CLARENDON
(looking off)
I see our friend Larry Mitchell is with us again.

Margo's hand stops in mid-air, holding mirror. She looks up
slowly.

MARGO
I couldn't care less.

Just the same, she sees in which direction Clarendon is
looking and starts to turn.

CLARENDON
And with a very beautiful girl, if my eyes don't
deceive me at this distance.

Margo reacts and swings around, CAMERA PANNING.
Larry and Betty have turned away from the desk and are
going towards elevators, bellhop behind them. Larry is
bending towards Betty intimately. Margo turns back to
Clarendon. Her face is frozen with a controlled emotion.

MARGO
I don't think I want any tea.

She picks up her bag and stands up. Goes out of shot.
Clarendon looks after her with a malicious smile.

DISSOLVE TO

8    INTERIOR. LIVING ROOM OF MARGO'S SUITE

It is very spacious, obviously very expensive. It is empty at
the moment. Margo unlocks door from outside, comes in,
shuts and locks door, walks swiftly into room, throws her bag
viciously on the desk, yanks her hat off, throws it on chair.
She goes over to the open balcony window, takes cigarette
out of box on desk, her hand shakes as she lights it with
lighter. She puffs at it furiously, looking out of window. After
a moment, she snubs it out in an ash tray, moves across to
telephone, picks it up.

MARGO
(into phone)
Mr. Larry Mitchell, please.
(pause—she changes her mind)
No. Never mind.

She puts telephone back in cradle and goes back to cigarette
box, lights another cigarette in the same nervous, jerky
manner, and puffs again. There is a KNOCK ON THE DOOR.
She spins around, walks quickly to door, throws it open.
Mitchell comes in. She says nothing as he moves in past her.
She shuts the door.

MITCHELL
I'm afraid you're not very glad to see me, Margo.

MARGO
(between her teeth)
With your charm? How could I help it? Have a nice trip?

MITCHELL
So-so.

MARGO
Who's the girl?

MITCHELL
Her name's Mayfield. Betty Mayfield.

MARGO
Nice.

MITCHELL
She's just a girl I met on the train. You don't mind, do you?

MARGO
(tartly)
Why should I mind?

MITCHELL
You shouldn't. You washed me up very thoroughly.

MARGO
As thoroughly as I could. It wasn't easy. But you are helping me.

MITCHELL
(staring at her)
Margo, darling. *You* washed *me* up. Remember? We're just friends. You wanted it that way.

MARGO
(ignoring this)
She's very beautiful. She's much younger than I am. And she's rich, I hope.

11

MITCHELL
Rich? I haven't the faintest idea. Why?

MARGO
You ought to know why.

MITCHELL
I don't. My hunch is she's just torn up an unhappy
marriage. I was able to do her a small favor.

MARGO
Splendid. Now she can return the compliment.

She crosses to a desk, gets her bag, gets keys out, unlocks the
desk drawer and jerks it open, takes something out and
turns, holding it in her hand. Two checks.

MARGO
She can give you enough money to cover these—
and the other bad checks you've given me.

Mitchell comes up to her slowly, looks down at the checks.

MITCHELL
I hoped to get enough to cover them before they
cleared. I wasn't lucky.

MARGO
You know what would happen to you if I turned
these over to the police?

MITCHELL
(quietly)
I have a rough idea.

MARGO
You'd go to jail. For quite a long term.

MITCHELL
Correct. I couldn't even afford to pay a lawyer to
defend me.

Pause. They stare at each other.

MITCHELL
What'll we do about it, Margo?


MARGO
She is much younger than I am. That's something
I'm going to have to get used to. Isn't it, Larry?
They'll all be much younger than I am. Here.
*(she holds out the checks)*
Tear them up.

He takes them, puts them in his pocket and stands there
looking at her. A sob catches in her throat.

MARGO
I guess I'm still in love with you, Larry. What an
idiot!

He reaches to take her in his arms. First she pushes him off,
then yields. He pulls her close and kisses her. Then, as they
come out of the kiss,

MITCHELL
I've always been a heel. I guess I always will be.


MARGO
You don't have to make a pose of it.


MITCHELL
It's the only pose I have left. I'm sunk. Broke. I
don't even have my hotel bill.

MARGO
*(a little sharply)*
I seem to recognize this routine. First the kiss.
Then the touch.

She makes a hopeless gesture.

MARGO
Oh, what's the use. You're you.

She turns and moves towards the desk.

MARGO
I only have a couple of hundred.

13

She picks her bag up, holds it out. He comes up beside her.

                    MARGO
    I seem to remember that you like to help yourself.

                    MITCHELL
                  (taking the bag)
        That's not very kind.

                    MARGO
    Kind or not kind. What's the difference? It always
    ends up the same way.

He gives her a twisted smile, opens the bag, rummages
through it, opens the zipper pocket inside and comes out
with some currency and looks it over, puts it in his pocket.
Puts the bag down on the desk, glances into the open drawer.
His look becomes fixed. What he sees, SHOOTING DOWN
INTO THE DRAWER, is a small, pearl-handled automatic,
lying in the corner. Mitchell's hand goes down into it, takes
the gun. TWO-SHOT of Margo and Mitchell as his hand
comes up with the gun.

                    MITCHELL
                  (almost amused)
        What's this?

                    MARGO
        What does it look like?

                    MITCHELL
        How long have you had it?

                    MARGO
        Years, why?

                    MITCHELL
    It's against the law to cross the border with a gun.
    The Canadian police might like to know about this.

                    MARGO
                  (very quietly)
        You already have the checks, darling.

                        14

MITCHELL
*(hurt)*
I didn't mean it that way.
*(he puts the gun back in the drawer,*
*pushes the drawer shut.)*
I'm sorry.

MARGO
Oh, forget it. Clark Brandon's throwing a party up
in his penthouse this evening. Take me?

MITCHELL
Of course.

MARGO
How about your new friend?

MITCHELL
*(with a laugh)*
I told you she's just—

MARGO
*(cutting in sharply)*
A girl you met on the train. Excuse my bringing it
up again.
*(she glances at her wrist watch)*
Be back in an hour. Right?

MITCHELL
Right.

He goes to take her in his arms again. This time she pushes
him away, quite gently, quite seriously.

MARGO
In an hour, Larry.

Mitchell stares at her levelly for a moment, then goes without
a word.

9     INTERIOR. CORRIDOR OUTSIDE MARGO'S ROOM

Mitchell has just closed her door, stands with his hand on the
knob, a smile playing across his features. He starts to whistle
as he walks down the corridor. He takes a little dance step

15

perhaps, this to indicate that his whole attitude with Margo is just part of an act. He stops beside a big sand jar, lights a cigarette, drops a match in jar, takes out the money from Margo's bag, flips it with a smile on his face, puts it back in his pocket, takes out the two checks Margo gave him, tears off the signatures, places checks in his pocket, tears the signature fragments into small pieces, drops them into the jar, goes on whistling.

DISSOLVE TO

10    INTERIOR. LOBBY—DESK AND ELEVATOR BANK

A couple of guests at the desk. A clerk is handing out mail. Campbell, the manager, is standing to one side. The elevator comes down. Mitchell comes out, crosses to the desk and addresses Campbell.

MITCHELL
Good afternoon, Mr. Campbell.

CAMPBELL
(coldly)
Mr. Mitchell.

MITCHELL
(airily)
A little something on account perhaps?

CAMPBELL
Rather more than a *little* something, Mr. Mitchell.

Mitchell takes money out of his pocket, puts it on the desk.

MITCHELL
I'm afraid this is all for the moment.

Campbell picks up the money, counts it, puts it down.

CAMPBELL
I think we'd better discuss this in my office, Mr. Mitchell.

MITCHELL
Nothing to discuss. Tomorrow the sun will shine even brighter. Be grateful for small mercies.

16

Campbell shrugs, reaches for the money.

                    MITCHELL
          Oh, I forgot. I have a dinner engagement. Excuse
          me.

He removes a couple of bills from the money.

                    MITCHELL
          Thank you, Mr. Campbell.

He puts money in his pocket, turns away. Campbell looks
after him with cold anger. Mitchell dodges back into elevator
just as it is about to start up.

11    INTERIOR. BETTY'S ROOM

Hat and suitcases in sight. Light is on in the closet. Betty is
inside closet, hanging up clothes. As she comes out, switch-
ing off light, DOOR BUZZER SOUNDS. She opens door.
Mitchell breezes on past her. She registers annoyance, then
closes door. Mitchell crosses to the open French door of the
balcony.

                    MITCHELL
          Nice room. Balcony and everything. Lovely view,
          too.

                    BETTY
                  (coolly)
          Very nice.

Mitchell turns.

                    MITCHELL
          No thanks?

                    BETTY
                (same voice)
          Thank you.

                    MITCHELL
                  (frowning)
          Suppose I hadn't known that immigration inspec-
          tor? Hadn't put in a good word for you?

17

BETTY
I'm supposing.

MITCHELL
I think you're a nice girl. I like you. But I can read signs if the print is large enough. It was your manner more than the wedding ring that bothered the inspector. A sort of tenseness, as if you were afraid of something.

Betty just goes on looking at him.

MITCHELL
I have a darned good idea your name isn't Betty Mayfield at all.

BETTY
Yes?

MITCHELL
How about taking Uncle Larry into the old firm? He's a useful guy to have on your side.

BETTY
(no answer)

MITCHELL
(slight change of pace)
Don't get me wrong, Betty. I'm not suggesting you murdered anybody, you know.

Betty reacts. He sees the reaction. His smile broadens. Then, very casually,

MITCHELL
Dine and dance tonight? I've got fifty bucks to throw away.

BETTY
Not tonight.

MITCHELL
What's the matter?

18

BETTY

I'm not in the mood for dining and dancing.

MITCHELL

We have some nice places around Vancouver.

BETTY

I'm sure you have.

MITCHELL
*(puzzled a little)*
Well, how about a breeze up to the penthouse about six o'clock? A friend of mine is throwing a cocktail party up there.

BETTY

I haven't been invited.

MITCHELL

Nobody gets invited to Clark Brandon's parties. They just go.

BETTY

Perhaps I'd better get you straightened out, Mr. Mitchell. You've been rather nice to me, in a couple of ways. And I'm grateful. But I don't think this entitles you to put me on a leash.

MITCHELL

Nobody I'd rather have on a leash.

Betty crosses to the door and opens it.

BETTY

I'm awfully sorry, but I'd like to take a bath and get freshened up.

Mitchell hesitates, then comes across slowly to the door.

MITCHELL

The brush-off, huh?

19

BETTY

I'm trying very hard to be polite about it.

Mitchell grins, then suddenly reaches for her and kisses her. She doesn't struggle, is quite impassive. After a moment he lets go, steps back.

MITCHELL

Don't I even get my face slapped?

BETTY
(indicating the open door)

Would you mind?

MITCHELL
(a little puzzled, confused by her attitude)

O.K. You win.

He starts out, turns to say,

MITCHELL

If you change your mind about the cocktail party— or anything else—give me a buzz.

BETTY

*If* I change my mind.

He goes. He closes the door. CAMERA MOVES IN ON HER FACE. She wipes off her lips with her handkerchief, almost in an absentminded way. The kiss didn't mean anything to her, one way or another. There is great loneliness in her eyes.

FADE OUT

FADE IN

12    WIDE SHOT—INTERIOR—LOBBY—VANCOUVER ROYAL

Showing a lot of activity, etc. The time is 6:00 P.M., approximately, but this is June in Canada and broad daylight, and will be for several hours yet. In the background Betty comes in through glass doors from the garden terrace, walks slowly across the lobby. People are looking at her with interest, especially the men. As she reaches the elevator bank, she glances off to one side, past the desk. Her look becomes fixed.

CAMERA PANS AROUND TO SHOW A NEON SIGN "TAVERN" this side of an archway, and people going in. She turns away from elevator, starts in that direction, passes on beneath sign.

13     INTERIOR. VANCOUVER ROYAL TAVERN

As Betty comes in, stands looking around. It is lighted somewhat dimly. There are a number of small tables. There is a bar but it is only for the use of the waiters. Betty looks around for a vacant table, then starts moving along looking for one. None empty, but at one sits a man alone. He is about 35, clean fine-drawn type, with a saturnine expression. He glances up. Betty meets his eyes, starts to turn away. Man indicates the empty chair opposite him. His manner of doing this is so completely indifferent to her as a person, that she hesitates.

                    BRANDON
                  (standing up)
You can have the table yourself, if you'd rather. I'm only killing time.

                    BETTY
No, please.

                    BRANDON
Sit down then. We often have to double up here.

                    BETTY
I see.

She pulls the chair back, sits down. Brandon sits down. He lights a cigarette, doesn't offer her one. She is watching him, a little puzzled, probably has had very few experiences of men not trying to pick her up in such circumstances. Betty looks around at the scurrying waiters who pay no attention to her yet.

                    BRANDON
                (calling out sharply)
Oh waiter.

Waiter turns, sees him, immediately comes to stand at his side.

21

                    WAITER
Yes sir.

Brandon, without speaking, indicates Betty. Waiter turns to
her.

                    WAITER
Yes, Miss.

                    BETTY
I'd like a dry martini. Very dry, please.

                    WAITER
Sorry, Miss. Beer and ale only. Canadian law.

                    BETTY
                  (surprised)
Beer?
                  (she shrugs)
Well—all right.

                    WAITER
Beer or ale, Miss?

                    BETTY
Ale. I don't mind.

                    WAITER
Right, Miss.

He turns away. Brandon is smiling at her faintly. She meets
his eyes, smiles back.

                    BETTY
                  (to Brandon)
Your liquor laws—

                    BRANDON
                  (cutting in)
Disgusting, aren't they? If you really want a
martini, I know where you can get one.

Betty looks inquiringly at him and doesn't speak.

                        22

BRANDON

A fellow named Brandon has a penthouse here. He's holding open-house. I was up there. Too noisy. Bored.

BETTY

I see.

BRANDON
(indifferently)
It might be worth a martini to you.

BETTY

I don't need it that badly. I don't enjoy crashing other people's parties.

BRANDON

It's open-house. No crashing involved. Anybody in the hotel's welcome.

BETTY

What did you say his name was?

BRANDON

Brandon. Clark Brandon. Fellow about my age. Lot of money—that he didn't make. Former American. Now naturalized in Canada. Social standing indeterminate. Manners not quite perfect. Scotch superb.

BETTY

You don't sound as if you liked him very well.

BRANDON
(quietly)
No—not very well. And I like his friends even less. But—
(he waves his hand indifferently)
If you really want a good dry martini—

BETTY

As I said before—

23

BRANDON

Sure. But I'd hate like the dickens to be held to everything I've said before, wouldn't you?

Betty suddenly laughs. The waiter brings the glass and the bottle of Bass ale, sets them down in front of her. Brandon makes a motion and the waiter goes away without collecting.

BETTY

You're not paying for this. It's quite enough that you let me sit at your table.

BRANDON

I never pay for anything. They just keep me here to amuse the guests.

BETTY

And *do* you amuse the guests?

BRANDON

No.
                    (indicating her bottle of ale)
Are you really going to drink that stuff?

BETTY

*You're* drinking it.

BRANDON

                    (indicating his almost untouched glass)
I can be talked out of it. As a matter of fact, I'd like a dry martini myself.

BETTY

Would it make you any more amusing?

BRANDON

Whatever you say.

BETTY

I didn't say anything.

BRANDON
*(standing up and putting money on the table)*
I don't know you and you don't know me. I made
a reasonably polite suggestion. But I'm sure you'd
rather be alone.

BETTY
I hate to be alone. But I've heard all the approaches
there are—even yours.

Brandon turns back, stares down at her coldly.

BRANDON
Neatly said—but to the wrong man. The trouble
with pretty girls is that they can't imagine anyone
thinking of anything else but the fact that they are
pretty girls. I get a little tired of it.

BETTY
*(directly)*
Do you think *I* don't?

BRANDON
*(interested)*
Thanks for the fresh air. That felt good.

BETTY
*(standing up and taking her bag)*
You're sure Mr. Brandon won't mind?

BRANDON
He doesn't even know half the people who come
up to drink his liquor.

DISSOLVE TO

14      EXTERIOR. LOBBY—OUTSIDE BRANDON'S PENTHOUSE

As elevator comes up. Brandon and Betty come out. There is
a sound of revelry behind the penthouse door, opposite the
elevators. They cross. Brandon opens the door casually,
without bothering to ring, ushers Betty in.

15      INTERIOR. LIVING ROOM—PENTHOUSE

A big room, with French doors opening on a large terrace. A
few couples are dancing outside on the terrace and a few
more inside the room. There is a portable bar at one side of

the room and two waiters behind it. The dance music is coming from a large radio-phonograph. Brandon and Betty come in. Brandon shuts the door. There are eighteen or twenty people around, with the usual alcoholic glitter in their eyes and the usual strident voices and exaggerated laughter. CAMERA PANS BRANDON AND BETTY OVER TOWARDS THE BAR, DISCOVERING Mitchell leaning against it, staring morosely into a drink. He drains the last of it.

                    MITCHELL
            *(to bartender in a thick voice)*
    Another.

Bartender takes his glass. Brandon and Betty come up to the bar. Mitchell does not at first look up.

                    BRANDON
                *(to bartender)*
    This lady would like a nice dry martini. So would I.

                    BARTENDER
    Very good, sir.

He turns away. Mitchell looks up, sees Betty, reacts.

                    MITCHELL
    Well well. Baby wouldn't come with me. Where
    did *you* pick her up?

Brandon glances from Betty to Mitchell puzzled, shrugs.

                    BRANDON
    Hello, Mitchell. Having fun?

                    MITCHELL
    The liquor's lovely. The rest of the party you can
    have.

He moves towards Betty, puts an arm around her. Betty tries to pull away.

                    MITCHELL
    What's the matter, baby? Don't you like me any
    more?

26

> BRANDON
> *(to Mitchell)*
> Lay off, can't you?

> MITCHELL
> Lay off what? This is my new girl friend. Met her
> on the train. She's very fond of me. Love at first
> sight. Wasn't it, baby?

Brandon reacts. There is a certain contempt in his look at
Betty now. Bartender serves drinks impassively. Mitchell
grabs his, gulps half of it down. Betty quietly releases herself
and moves away from him.

> BRANDON
> *(to Betty)*
> And I'd begun to think this was my lucky day.

A liveried hotel servant COMES INTO SHOT.

> SERVANT
> *(to Brandon)*
> You're wanted on the telephone, Mr. Brandon.
> Mrs. West.

As the servant says "Brandon," Betty reacts.

> BRANDON
> *(to servant)*
> Thanks.
> *(to Betty with brutal sarcasm)*
> If you are a friend of Larry Mitchell's, I'm sure I
> leave you in good hands.

He goes out of SHOT. She looks after him unhappily.
CAMERA PANS BRANDON across his living room to an
inner door. He starts through.

16      INTERIOR. BEDROOM

Telephone on table, receiver down as Brandon enters, closes
door against the noise.

> BRANDON
> *(into phone)*
> Hello Margo. Aren't you coming up?

27

> *(pause)*
> Mitchell? Oh yes, he's here.
> *(he smiles a little grimly)*
> He came up alone, but it seems he has a new girl friend with him now.
> *(pause)*
> Don't be theatrical, Margo. What do you care about Mitchell? Come on up and have a drink.

17    INTERIOR—MARGO'S LIVING ROOM

Margo on phone.

> MARGO
> *(in a flat voice)*
> I haven't any intention of being theatrical. Of course I'll come up. Goodbye.

She hangs up, stands a moment, staring at nothing, then she turns, picks her wrap out of the chair, puts it on, crosses to the desk for her handbag. She opens the bag, pauses, then in slow motion, pulls open the drawer of the desk. CAMERA IN A CLOSE SHOT, studies her face as she looks down into the drawer of the desk, which we do not see. But we already know there is a gun there. Her body is quite motionless, her expression frozen. When she moves we do not see whether she takes the gun out of the drawer or not. We hear the snap of her bag shutting. Then she turns away, starts across the room to leave.

DISSOLVE TO

18    INTERIOR—ELEVATOR IN MOTION UP

A quiet, gentlemanly-looking man is leaning against the back wall of the elevator, wearing a trench coat and a soft hat. He is a homicide dick named *Killaine*, but you'd never think that to look at him. Elevator stops, doors open, and Margo enters.

> ELEVATOR BOY
> *(very polite)*
> Did you have a nice day, Mrs. West?

> MARGO
> I had a rotten day, if it's any of your business.

ELEVATOR BOY

I'm terribly sorry, Mrs. West.

MARGO

Don't let it break you up.

ELEVATOR BOY

Oh, I wouldn't do that, Mrs. West.

The man chuckles. Margo looks around at him.

MARGO

What's so funny?

Killaine wipes the smile off his face.

KILLAINE
(imitating boy)

I'm terribly sorry, Mrs. West.

As she stares at him, he takes his monocle out of his pocket, polishes it, sticks it in his eye.

MARGO

Oh, the Coldstream Guards.
(pause)
Don't you take your hat off in elevators?

KILLAINE
(pleasantly)

I never wear a hat.
(his face changes to consternation)
Oh, so I am. I forgot—
(he takes his hat off)
I guess I'm terribly sorry again, Mrs. West.

Elevator stops.

ELEVATOR BOY

Penthouse floor, please.

Margo sweeps out, Killaine follows her.

19    EXTERIOR—LOBBY

As they cross to the penthouse door.

KILLAINE

May I?

He pushes the button.

MARGO

May you what?

KILLAINE

Oh nothing.

MARGO

Are you always this witty?

Killaine laughs as the door opens. Brandon stands in it.

BRANDON

Hi Margo. Hello, Killaine. You two come together?

MARGO

In the same elevator. It is a public conveyance.

CAMERA TAKES THEM INTO THE ROOM. The door starts to close.

20    INTERIOR OF BRANDON'S LIVING ROOM

Brandon, Killaine and Margo standing by the door.

BRANDON

Let me introduce you. Mr. Killaine, Mrs. West.

MARGO
(not looking at Killaine)

Fascinated.

Her eyes roam the room. She picks out Mitchell. Her expression freezes. WHAT SHE SEES: Betty is sitting in her chair in a corner and Mitchell is standing over her, his hand on the back of the chair. Her expression is wooden. His is a mixture of insolence and pleading. CAMERA RETURNS TO MARGO, BRANDON AND KILLAINE as they cross to the bar. At the same time Mitchell leaves Betty, also crosses to the bar, reaches it about the same time as Margo. Margo gives Mitchell a long, cool, empty stare. Mitchell smiles a little sheepishly, embarrassed even in his drunkenness.

30

BRANDON

What'll you have, Margo?


MARGO
*(without looking at him)*

Martini.


BRANDON
*(to Killaine)*

You, Killaine?


KILLAINE

Scotch and plain water, I think.


MARGO
*(not looking at him)*

Warm water, no doubt.


BRANDON

What?


KILLAINE

A private joke.

He gets the monocle out and sticks it in his eye again.


KILLAINE

It goes with this—cold houses and warm drinks—
the effete Englishman.


BRANDON

You're not English.

Bartender serves drinks. Margo puts her bag down on the
bar. It makes a heavy clunking sound. Killaine's eyes go to it,
without too much expression. Mitchell reacts more. To him
the clunking sound has a meaning. He starts to reach for the
bag. Margo pointedly moves it away from him.


MITCHELL
*(to Margo thickly)*

I'm sorry. I forgot about calling for you.

31

MARGO

It's quite unimportant, Mr. Mitchell. After all, you got what you wanted.

MITCHELL

Be nasty.

MARGO

I have no intention of being nasty, Mr. Mitchell.

MITCHELL

In that case, there's someone here I'd like to introduce you to. Over there.

Margo looks towards Betty. She reacts.

MARGO
*(almost to herself)*
She is beautiful. And young.
*(she turns back to Mitchell)*
No thank you.

MITCHELL
*(aggressively)*
I say YES.

MARGO
*(quietly turning her back on him and reaching for her glass)*
You're not the type to be masterful, darling. It takes character.

Mitchell reaches for her shoulder and spins her around, causing her to slop some of her drink out on the bar.

MARGO
*(with sudden deadly sweetness)*
Of course, darling. Anything you say.

She goes off with Mitchell. Killaine looks after them puzzled. Brandon is indifferent.

KILLAINE

That's what I like about cocktail parties. Everyone is so perfectly natural.

32

                              BRANDON
        How's life treating you?

                              KILLAINE
        The usual grind.

                              BRANDON
        Round of golf Saturday?

                              KILLAINE
        If I can get off.

21      CORNER OF THE ROOM

        Betty is sitting alone as Margo and Mitchell COME INTO
        SHOT.

                              MITCHELL
        Betty, this is Margo West. She wants to meet you.
        Miss Mayfield.

                              BETTY
        How do you do?

                              MARGO
                         (staring at her)
        You're very attractive, my dear. And you look very
        unsophisticated.

                              MITCHELL
        Unsophisticated.
                         (he laughs nastily)
        If you knew about this babe—

        Betty stands up quickly.

                              BETTY
        I think I'd like to dance.

                              MITCHELL
        Why certainly, baby.

        He puts his arm around Betty and dances off with her, leaving
        Margo standing. CAMERA FOLLOWS THEM as they dance.
        They pass Mr. Clarendon, who is sitting as usual with his

silver-knobbed cane between his legs, paying no particular attention to anything.

> BETTY
> *(to Mitchell as they dance)*
> Please be a little more careful how you talk, Mr. Mitchell.

> MITCHELL
> How careful should I be?

> BETTY
> I don't like being referred to as a babe, or addressed as baby. I don't like your possessive attitude, nor your hints of secret knowledge. In fact, to be very frank, Mr. Mitchell, I don't think I like you.

> MITCHELL
> Maybe you're going to have to like me.

He disengages her left hand enough to hold it up and look at it.

> MITCHELL
> You've shed the ring, haven't you? Took my advice. That's the girl. Keep right on taking my advice and we'll get somewhere.

Betty jerks away from him and stops.

> BETTY
> I think you're drunk.

> MITCHELL
> Just drunk enough.

He puts his arm around her, pulls her close to him, and tilts her head back. She struggles against him, silently. He pushes her head back farther and kisses her solidly on the mouth. She finally breaks away from him with flashing eyes.

> MITCHELL
> What's the matter, baby? Don't you like being kissed?

                    BETTY
                *(with cold fury)*
Next time you try that, Mr. Mitchell—
*(pause, she takes a deep breath, then very pointedly)*
—don't. I'm warning you.

Brandon and Margo COME INTO THE SHOT from different
directions.


                   BRANDON
Do me a favor, Mitchell. Find yourself a nice
secluded park bench.

                   MITCHELL
                   *(airily)*
Did I do something wrong?

                   BRANDON
I wouldn't know. Just do it somewhere else. There
*is* such a thing as good manners.

                   MITCHELL
How would *you* know, Brandon?

                   BRANDON
                  *(harshly)*
Want to walk out—or get thrown out?

                   MITCHELL
You don't throw guests out, Brandon.

                   BRANDON
Don't bet on it. I'm eccentric.

The two men glare at each other. Mitchell finally shrugs, then
goes towards the door.


                    MARGO
             *(to Brandon, quietly)*
It takes two to make a clinch, Clark. Nice to have
seen you.

She starts towards the door. Brandon hurries quickly to open
it for her. She goes out without looking at him, her mouth

tight. He shuts the door, looks back towards Betty, who has remained standing perfectly still. She takes a handkerchief out of her bag and scrubs her mouth off as Brandon comes back to her. Clarendon stands up slowly.

> BRANDON
> *(to Betty, offhand)*
>
> Dance?

> BETTY
>
> No thank you.

> CLARENDON
> *(to Brandon)*
> Where I come from, Mr. Brandon, the host tries to protect his guests from insult.

> BRANDON
>
> I stopped him.

> CLARENDON
> And if he fails, he at least has the good manners to apologize.

> BRANDON
> I don't exactly regard Larry Mitchell's pick-ups—

Clarendon turns his back on him. Then,

> CLARENDON
> *(to Betty, with a courtly gesture)*
> We haven't been introduced. But if you'll overlook that, I'm sure that between us we can contrive a graceful exit.

> BETTY
> *(smiling at him warmly)*
> Thank you very much.

They go towards the door side by side. Brandon turns and CAMERA PANS HIM BACK TO BAR where Killaine has remained motionless, his drink untasted.

BRANDON
Would it have helped if I'd knocked him down?

KILLAINE
Hardly. Who's the girl?

BRANDON
Somebody Mitchell picked up on the train. I don't
even know her name.

KILLAINE
She doesn't look like a girl who would let herself
be picked up on a train.

BRANDON
That's what I thought, at first.
(pause)
Maybe somebody else ought to have thrown this
party.
(pause)
With my liquor of course.

DISSOLVE TO

22    CLOSE SHOT

Face of traveling clock on night table. Room is dark, lit only
by moonlight. Hands of the clock stand at almost 11:15.
Ticking is HEARD faintly. A little smoke drifts across the face
of the clock. CAMERA PANS BACK ALONG THE SMOKE to
Betty lying in bed, her eyes wide open. Somewhere outside a
church clock chimes the quarter hour. The last strokes of the
chime are drowned out by a sudden peal of thunder. Betty
jerks upright in bed. The thunder frightens her. There is
another louder peal, this time preceded by a flash of lightning
which lights up her face. She shuts her eyes against it. The
thunderstorm grows suddenly heavy. Repeated flashes of
lightning across her face and peals of thunder. CAMERA
MOVES IN ON HER EYES which are frozen.

23    CAMERA PULLS BACK VERY SLOWLY

and everything has changed except Betty's expression. The
flashes go on, but they are now seen to be the flashbulbs of

newspaper cameramen. Betty is dressed very soberly and is standing just inside the door of a courtroom with a jail matron beside her. The CAMERA KEEPS ON PULLING BACK, AWAY FROM BETTY, and the entire courtroom is seen. It is late at night in the county courthouse GREENWATER, NORTH CAROLINA. There is an excited buzzing of conversation. A Bailiff is rapping for order. The jury is sitting, grim-faced and silent, in the box. The Judge is not on the bench yet. Betty is led along the side corridor then through the bar where the defense attorney, a haggard, dark-haired young man, stands waiting for her. (NOTE: All Southern accents except Betty's in this scene.)

BAILIFF
*(shouting)*
Everybody stand up! His Honor, Judge Hopkinson! Court now in session!

Everybody stands up. Betty and the jail matron and the young attorney face towards the bench. CAMERA SHOWS THE PROSECUTING ATTORNEY, also standing up at his table. CAMERA PANS OVER TO THE DOOR OF THE JUDGE'S CHAMBERS, as Judge Hopkinson comes into the courtroom. He walks slowly to the bench, stands a moment behind it, looking out over the courtroom, then sits down. He is a distinguished courtly Southerner of the best type, an old man but very erect. When he sits, all the spectators and lawyers sit down. The double doors at the back are closed and a Bailiff stands with his back to them. Suddenly, one of the doors is pushed open, almost knocking the Bailiff out of the way. He turns angrily as HENRY KINSOLVING enters. The Bailiff seeing who it is, stands aside. Henry Kinsolving is an arrogant, bitter man about 60 years old, with the stamp of power and authority. He marches down the center aisle of the court through the bar, and sits at the table near the Prosecutor. The Judge stares down at him coldly.

JUDGE
Mr. Bailiff, please make room for Mr. Henry Kinsolving outside the bar of the court.

Henry Kinsolving springs to his feet and glares at the Judge. Then he turns and goes back through the gate of the bar and sits down outside in a chair the Bailiff places for him solicitously. There is a general shuffling of feet and noise which subsides slowly.

JUDGE
*(slowly and impressively)*
Before the Jury renders its verdict, the Court
wishes to warn those present that there is to be no
demonstration of any kind. No person is to leave
the courtroom until the Court rises.
*(he glances towards press table)*
I repeat—no one is to leave the courtroom.

There is a silence, then the Judge turns towards the Clerk.

JUDGE
You may proceed, Mr. Clerk.

CLERK
*(he stands and looks at Elizabeth)*
The Defendant will rise and face the Jury.

Elizabeth stands up slowly and turns towards the Jury, who
do not look at her. They stare somewhere over her head. The
Clerk turns back to the Jury.

CLERK
Gentlemen of the Jury, have you reached a verdict?

FOREMAN
*(standing)*
We have.

CLERK
And what is your verdict?

FOREMAN
We the Jury, find the Defendant, Elizabeth Kinsolving, guilty of murder in the first degree.

There is a surge of noise in the well of the court. The Judge
raps sharply with his gavel. A couple of pressmen start to get
up, then look back and see that the doors are guarded and sit
down again. The Prosecutor looks grimly satisfied; he glances
at the defending counsel with a half smile. Defense Counsel,
whose name is LEAMINGTON, is shocked and pale. Eliza-

beth shows no reaction at all. Henry Kinsolving draws his mouth a little tighter, and there is a gleam in his eye. The spectators look, for the most part, very satisfied. Leamington comes to his feet.

LEAMINGTON
*(in a strangled voice)*
Motion to poll the Jury, if it please the Court.

JUDGE
So ordered.

The Clerk now proceeds to poll the Jury, saying, "Juror No. 1, what is your verdict?" and the Juror answering, "Guilty of murder in the first degree." "Juror No. 2, what is your verdict?" etc. This is covered by a series of CLOSEUPS. All answer clearly until Clerk comes to Juror No. 7, who mumbles in a low voice.

CLERK
*(to Juror No. 7)*
Speak a little louder, please.

Juror No. 7 is staring hard at Elizabeth. His face is twisted with emotion. He is the only Juror who has looked at her. He swallows, doesn't answer, then his eyes go to Henry Kinsolving. Henry Kinsolving glares at Juror No. 7. Juror No. 7 wilts.

JUROR NO. 7
*(thickly and hesitatingly)*
Guilty of murder in the first degree.

The Clerk completes the polling of the Jury, then turns to the Judge. The Judge nods and Clerk sits down. The courtroom starts to get noisy again, and the Judge uses his gavel.

BAILIFF
Order in the Court!

JUDGE
The Court now has a statement to make.

He glances towards Elizabeth, who is still standing rigidly.

40

JUDGE
*(gently)*
Please sit down, Mrs. Kinsolving.

Elizabeth sits, and clasps her hands in front of her.

JUDGE
This court, like most courts, has occasionally been
guilty of judicial error. Prior to the commencement
of this trial, Mr. Leamington, as attorney for the
Defendant, made a motion for a change of venue
on the ground that a fair trial could not be had by
this Defendant in this jurisdiction. Most of you
know why this motion was made. The Defendant
was alleged to have been tried and convicted in the
columns of the daily newspaper owned by her
father-in-law, Mr. Henry Kinsolving, and as a
result public opinion was said to have been preju-
diced to the extent that it was doubtful twelve
Jurors could be found with open minds. This
Court regretfully denied the motion. It did not
believe that a Jury with open minds could not be
found. The members of this Jury declared on oath
that their minds were open. The Court had no
reason at that time to disbelieve them.

The Judge looks at the Jury sternly, and they react in various
ways. The Judge's eyes go to Henry Kinsolving, who stares
back at him.

JUDGE
Elizabeth Kinsolving has been tried and found
guilty of the murder of her husband, Lee Kinsolving. Lee Kinsolving was the only son of our most
prominent citizen. Mr. Kinsolving controls, or is
said to control, our leading bank, many of our
business enterprises and our only daily newspaper. He affords employment to a large number of
our citizens. His influence on our affairs is very
great.
*(dramatic pause)*
Perhaps *too* great.

There is an upsurge of noise in the Court and the Bailiff
shouts for order. Prosecutor jumps to his feet.

41

PROSECUTOR
Your Honor, I protest that statement!

JUDGE
Sit down, Mr. Prosecutor. You are out of order.

Prosecutor swallows, looks back at Henry Kinsolving, shrugs and sits down again. Leamington is leaning forward with a gleam in his eye. Elizabeth is still deadpan.

JUDGE
We all knew Lee Kinsolving well. We watched him grow up. We observed that he was proud and hot-tempered, and had a strain of arrogance, not unlike others of his family.
    (he looks meaningly at Henry Kinsolving)
From this town Lee Kinsolving went to fight for his country. And to this town, before he went over-seas, he brought the wife he had married up North. To us he returned a war hero badly wounded, condemned for the rest of his life to wear a heavy brace around his neck. Competent medical testimony has shown that without that brace a very slight movement might have been enough to snap his spinal cord. This injury humiliated and embittered Lee Kinsolving, made him morose and violent, and perhaps caused him to drink to excess. The Defendant has admitted that there were bitter quarrels between herself and her husband. Such a quarrel took place on the night of his death. Upon the manner of that death this entire proceeding rests.

The Judge pauses and looks out over the courtroom, which is very quiet now. He pours himself a glass of water and takes a drink from it.

JUDGE
In my summing up to the Jury I emphasized that the case for the prosecution was, as so many murder cases are, purely circumstantial. It was alleged that while Lee Kinsolving slept, perhaps in a drunken stupor and perhaps not, the Defendant

42

removed the neck brace from his neck and jerked his head sufficiently to rupture the spinal cord and cause his death. It is admitted that the Defendant was found holding the neck brace in her hand, and bending over her husband's body, which was lying *on* the bed. Not *in* the bed, mind you, but sprawled across it. The Defendant has testified that Lee Kinsolving himself removed the neck brace to torment her, as it were, with the great danger in which this placed him.

That he then started to walk towards her, holding the brace in his hands, and that being unsteady on his feet, he stumbled and fell backwards across the bed. And that this fall broke his neck, although at the time she did not know it. She has testified that she picked the brace up from the floor and was about to attempt to replace it on his neck when her father-in-law entered the room and found her in that position.

*(pause)*

By its verdict the Jury declared that Elizabeth Kinsolving's account of the death of her husband to be impossible of belief.

The Judge sips a little more water, then continues.

In all murder trials, a motion by the Defense for a directed verdict of acquittal before the case goes to the Jury is more or less automatic. It is usually perfunctory, and for that reason immediately denied. The laws of this state, and of a few other jurisdictions, confer upon a Court a right to reserve its ruling upon such a motion until after the Jury has rendered its verdict. In this proceeding, I, as presiding Judge, availed myself of this power. I most honestly hoped that the Jury in this case might act as impartially as it declared itself to be.

The Prosecuting Attorney again jumps to his feet, then changes his mind, sits down with a frustrated angry movement. Kinsolving is leaning forward, glaring. The Jury are now very uncomfortable. There is a BUZZ OF NOISE and the Bailiff again shouts for order.

43

## JUDGE

Let me remind you that a Jury is the sole judge of
fact, and further let me remind you that the Jury
must judge all the facts. It may not select nor create
nor change facts. It may only interpret them. It
may not declare something impossible which in
fact is merely extremely difficult to believe.

*(pause)*

Impossible is a very big word.

*(another pause)*

If we are to believe Elizabeth Kinsolving's sworn
testimony, we must also believe that Lee's Kinsolving performed an act which was almost certain to
cause his death. It is difficult—*very* difficult to
believe. But is it *impossible*? Are we sure that he
*knew* it would cause his death? Or that in his then
state of mind, he even considered the conse-
quences at all? Many people have attempted suicide as a result of domestic quarrels. Not all have
succeeded, nor meant to succeed. And surely not
all of those who *did* succeed—fully intended to.
Not all knew what they were doing, and of those
who did know, there were surely a few whose
desire to hurt others overcame their fear of hurting
themselves. We cannot know what was in Lee
Kinsolving's mind. Therefore, some element of
doubt must infallibly remain. It was not necessary
for this Jury to declare its belief in the Defendant's
innocence, nor to declare that Lee Kinsolving died
by accident or his own intent. It *was* necessary for
the Jury to admit to themselves, as reasonable
men, the possibility—however slight—that Elizabeth Kinsolving's story was true. This possibility
the Jury has refused to admit.

*(dramatic pause)*

It therefore becomes my duty to declare that such a
possibility does in fact exist—and that the Jury's
refusal to recognize it was a failure to exercise its
proper function.

A rising, antagonistic sound begins to surge from the
spectators and Henry Kinsolving comes to his feet, slowly
and rigidly. The Judge ignores him and looks straight at the

foreman of the Jury, and speaks the rest of this speech in a clear, ringing, dominating voice.

JUDGE

The Court therefore rules that the motion of the Attorney for the Defense for a directed verdict of not guilty be now granted. The verdict of guilty brought in by this Jury is hereby set aside, and a verdict of not guilty is to be entered on the record.
*(his voice now rises almost to a shout)*
And the Defendant, Elizabeth Kinsolving, is herewith discharged from the custody of the Sheriff of this county.

PANDEMONIUM and UPROAR in the Court. The Bailiff shouts for order. The Judge stands up slowly, looks a moment out over the Court, then looks at Elizabeth, smiles at her faintly, turns, and starts back towards his chambers. CAMERA PANS over to Henry Kinsolving. He stands like a statue, in icy rage, his face working, while behind him the noise of the spectators goes on. Kinsolving turns his head towards Elizabeth, then moves stiffly over to her, CAMERA PANNING. He comes up close to her. Leamington, the Defense Attorney, and the matron are standing beside her.

KINSOLVING
*(with restrained fury)*
For four years I endured your presence in my house, although I well knew you were no fit wife for my son—that he had married in haste, and that he would repent it bitterly, if he survived the war. I had no thought that he would die under his own roof, nor that the reward of my patience would be to stand beside his grave. I have done my best to avenge him. So far I have failed. But I have not finished. You are free to go where you will, but there will be another day of reckoning, somewhere, sometime. And when that day comes, I will be there. And that time you will not escape.

Elizabeth's eyes widen with horror. In the background the crowd is still roaring, like peals of thunder. CAMERA

MOVES IN CLOSE TO ELIZABETH'S EYES as at the beginning of this flashback.

24      CAMERA WITHDRAWS and finds her sitting up in bed in the Vancouver Royal Hotel. Thunder is pealing outside, but now more distantly. There is a sudden downpour of rain. Betty sweeps the bedclothes aside, reaches for a robe, and crosses to close the French doors. Over her shoulder we see a portion of the small balcony, a chaise, and as Betty starts to close the door, she stops frozen. There is someone lying on the chaise. She starts out into the rain.

25      EXTERIOR—BALCONY

As she comes out, approaches the chaise, leans down, the rain beating on her. She shakes the shoulder of a man on the chaise. He doesn't move. One of his hands drops limply and swings a little. Horror shows in Betty's eyes. She reaches out and touches the man's face, and we see for the first time that this is Larry Mitchell, and we realize that he is dead.

VERY SLOW DISSOLVE TO

26      THE PORTER'S DESK ON THE CORRIDOR OF THE MAIN FLOOR OF THE HOTEL

The night porter is seated at his desk, reading a paper. He is a middle-aged man in uniform and military bearing, with a row of ribbons across his chest. Probably, in order of seniority, a Military Medal, a Good Conduct Medal, the Long Service Medal, and two or three campaign ribbons. Betty, now fully dressed, COMES SLOWLY INTO THE SHOT and stops by his desk. Porter lays down his paper and stands up.

PORTER
Good evening, Miss.

BETTY
How soon can I get a plane to Seattle?

PORTER
I'm afraid there's nothing more tonight, miss. Unless you charter a plane.

46

BETTY

How long would that take?

PORTER

Well—they have to service the plane—and get a
pilot down to the field, unless there's one hanging
around there still—and then they have to get the
immigration officer—

BETTY

Immigration officer?

PORTER

Crossing the border this time of night they're a bit
particular. You'd have to prove your identity, you
know—unless you've got a passport. They might
even want to know why you're in such a hurry.
(he grins)
Otherwise, they might think—

He breaks off, staring at her.

BETTY
(quietly)
They might think I was running away from something.

PORTER

Possibly, miss.
(he smiles)

BETTY

Thank you very much.

She turns and exits. CAMERA FOLLOWS HER ALONG. She
turns the corner by the elevator bank, starts into elevator.
Brandon is standing there in a light overcoat, with his hat in
his hand. She gets in without noticing him.

27    INTERIOR OF ELEVATOR IN MOTION

BRANDON

Leaving us so soon, Miss Mayfield?

She realizes his presence.

47

BRANDON
I don't blame you—for running away.

Betty reacts sharply, controls herself, says nothing. Elevator
stops, doors open.

ELEVATOR BOY
Good night, miss.

BETTY
Good night.

She starts out, Brandon after her.

ELEVATOR BOY
This isn't the penthouse floor, Mr. Brandon.

Brandon keeps going.

28    INTERIOR OF CORRIDOR OUTSIDE ELEVATOR

Betty is walking quickly down corridor towards her room.
Brandon is following her. She seems unaware of him.

BRANDON
(calling)
Miss Mayfield—

Betty stops, turns, and he comes up to her.

BRANDON
I know it's a little late for an apology.

BETTY
(in a strained, unnatural voice)
Much too late.

BRANDON
Don't take it so big—it isn't a tragedy.

Betty goes into a peal of hysterical laughter. Brandon grabs
hold of her arm and shakes it.

BRANDON
What's the matter with you?

Betty stops laughing just as suddenly as she began.

48

> BETTY
> You said it wasn't a tragedy.

> BRANDON
> What's funny about that? If you pick up with people like Larry Mitchell, other people are bound to get funny ideas about you. The world is full of Larry Mitchells.

> BETTY
> There's one less tonight.

Brandon reacts. Silently she holds out a key. He takes it. It's a tabbed hotel room key.

QUICK DISSOLVE TO

29   INTERIOR OF BETTY'S ROOM AS DOOR OPENS

Brandon comes in, stands aside as Betty comes in. He shuts and locks the door. The room is lighted up. Brandon looks around swiftly.

> BETTY
> Out on the balcony.

CAMERA PANS Brandon across the room to the balcony door. He steps out.

30   EXTERIOR OF BALCONY AS BRANDON ENTERS

He goes quickly to chaise, stares down, bends, appears to pick something up. What it is is not seen.

31   INTERIOR OF BETTY'S ROOM AS BRANDON ENTERS

Betty is standing motionless in the middle of the floor.

> BRANDON
> Through the heart, apparently. Very little blood. What's the story?

Betty looks him straight in the eye.

> BETTY
> There isn't one—that anyone would believe. I went for a walk after dinner, down to the ocean—

alone. I came up and went to bed. I didn't sleep very well. Then there was a thunderstorm. And it began to rain. I went across to close the French door. That's the first time I saw him out there.

                    BRANDON
He got in here how?

                    BETTY
Not with my consent, strange as it seems. I don't know how he got in. I don't know anything.

Brandon brings his hand up.

                    BRANDON
Ever see this before?

Betty looks down. In his hand is an automatic with a pearl handle.

                    BETTY
No. And I've never fired a gun in my life. Aren't you supposed not to touch it?

                    BRANDON
Sure—but somebody always does.

He puts the gun down on the table carelessly, gets out a cigarette case and offers her one. She takes it and he lights it for her. Her hand is shaky. Their faces are very close together. He holds the lighter close to her eyes.

                    BRANDON
                    (quietly)
Lovely eyes—honest eyes—

The light goes out.

                    BRANDON
They'll know whether he killed himself.

                    BETTY
I don't.

BRANDON

How did you meet him?


BETTY

On the train. He said he lived here, and he offered
to make a reservation for me.


BRANDON

Nice of him.


BETTY

He knew the immigration officer. He eased himself
in.


BRANDON

He was a great boy for that. What else?


BETTY

That's all there is.

Brandon takes her by the shoulders and pulls her close,
looking into her eyes.


BRANDON

They're still honest eyes—but there's something
behind them.

He pulls her closer, about to kiss her.


BETTY

Go ahead—if you want to. It doesn't matter.


BRANDON

I'd rather wait until it does matter.

He lets go of her and starts across the room, picks up
telephone. Brandon turns with the telephone in his hand.


BRANDON

You tried to run away.


BETTY

There wasn't any plane.

51

BRANDON

It's always a mistake to run away. *Always.*

He begins to dial.

FADE OUT

FADE IN

32    INTERIOR. BRANDON'S LIVING ROOM—NIGHT

Brandon is standing at the French window, a cup of coffee in his hand. CAMERA PULLS BACK AS his eyes go over to Betty who is in a chair with an untouched cup of black coffee on the table beside her.

BRANDON
*(going towards her)*
Want a spike in it?

BETTY
*(without looking at him)*
No thanks.

Her voice and expression are dead and exhausted. CAMERA PULLS BACK FURTHER to show Margo and Clarendon sitting across the room from Betty. Margo is staring at Betty with cold hostility. She is wearing slacks, but otherwise dressed with care and finish. Clarendon is fully dressed and has his silver-topped cane between his legs, but has slippers on his feet.

MARGO
You make friends quickly, don't you, Clark?

BRANDON
Sometimes.

MARGO
And without much discrimination.

BRANDON
Leave that one lay.

MARGO
They still hang women in Canada, I've heard.

52

CLARENDON
So much less refined than frizzling them in the
electric chair.

MARGO
Oh, shut up!
*(she looks down at his feet)*
You haven't even got your spats on.

Brandon crosses to coffee table, picks up coffee pot and goes
to Margo with it.

MARGO
Think I'll have trouble staying awake?

Brandon fills her cup silently. Margo chokes, bites on her
handkerchief hard. She controls herself.

MARGO
I'm sorry. This thing has just about knocked me
silly. How long do we have to wait for this police
character?

BRANDON
Until he comes. He's a nice guy. You've met him.

Margo and Clarendon both react, staring. Brandon takes half
dollar out of his pocket and sticks it in his eye.

MARGO
That comedian?

Betty is looking across at Brandon with sudden interest.

BRANDON
Don't let the eyeglass fool you. That's what it's for.

DOOR BUZZER SOUNDS. Brandon crosses to open door. A
plainclothes dick named Handley is standing there.

HANDLEY
You Mr. Brandon?

Brandon nods.

HANDLEY

Inspector Killaine's compliments. He'll be up in another ten minutes.

Brandon nods again, and as Handley starts to turn away, Brandon starts to close door.

CUT TO

33     EXTERIOR. BALCONY OUTSIDE BETTY'S ROOM—NIGHT

Portable lights have been rigged up and a police photographer is taking photographs of the body. As he finishes, a sheet is thrown over it and the photographer starts to dismantle his equipment and pack it up. A couple of plainclothes men are standing around, and one of them named Gore, a detective sergeant, a big sore-head who doesn't like anybody. As the photographer extinguishes one of the lights and starts to wind up the cord, Gore looks off and scowls. Killaine ENTERS THE SHOT briskly. He is wearing a trenchcoat and no hat.

GORE

You in charge here?

KILLAINE

So it seems, Sergeant.

GORE

Right.

KILLAINE

I hate to pull rank on you, Sergeant, but once in a while—for moral purposes—you might address me as "Inspector." In moments of extreme desperation, you might even call me "sir."

He goes over to chaise, lifts sheet off corpse, looks down, replaces sheet, comes back to Gore.

KILLAINE

I knew him. He was easy to dislike, poor chap.

54

GORE

They tell me he'll be a great loss to the liquor trade.
This Mayfield girl—
*(he breaks off as Killaine reacts)*
—I suppose you knew her, too, Inspector.

KILLAINE

I've met her.

GORE

It's her room. She only got to the hotel this
afternoon. With him.
*(he indicates body on chaise)*
I guess he took too much for granted. Here's the
gun.

He takes it out of his pocket and holds it out on a
handkerchief. Killaine takes the gun from him, handkerchief
and all.

KILLAINE

Pearl-handled .25 automatic, eh?
*(he looks a little closer)*
No, it's a Belgian gun—6.5 mm.

GORE

Correct, Inspector. A woman's gun. U.S. 125
caliber ammunition in it. It was on a table in there.

He nods towards room. Killaine frowns.

GORE

Nobody's been questioned yet. You noticed the
wound of entry?
*(Killaine nods)*
Much too low for a suicide. Not conclusive, of
course. But a woman of ordinary height, standing
rather close to a tall man, such as he was—
*(indicating corpse)*
—would be apt to shoot him just about where he
got shot.
*(Killaine nods again)*
Then there's the shell.

55

He takes out a small envelope, hands it to Killaine.

                              GORE
          This make of gun throws a shell backwards, high,
          and to the right. The chaise is only about four feet
          from the wall.

                            KILLAINE
          So the shell ought to have gone over?

                              GORE
          Unless the gun was slanted up.

                            KILLAINE
          So the wound and the shell give you the same
          answer.

                              GORE
          Right. A clean deduction from observed facts.
          They've got to be simple *once* in a while, Inspector.

                            KILLAINE
                            (dryly)
          I've always looked forward to it. All right, let's get
          him out of here and tidy up.
                    (he starts to turn away)

                              GORE
          I'd take a look in her clothes closet if I were you,
          Inspector.

Killaine nods and exits scene.

34   INTERIOR OF BETTY'S ROOM AS KILLAINE ENTERS
     FROM BALCONY

He stands a moment, looking around, crosses to dressing
table, looks down, and we SEE traces of fingerprint powder
on the toilet articles and bottles. He doesn't touch anything.
He crosses to closet, opens door. A light goes on inside. He
starts in.

35   INTERIOR OF BETTY'S CLOSET

Killaine examines several garments, takes a sports coat off
hanger, opens it up, looks at lining. His look becomes fixed

and intent. He reacts. (What he sees is that the sewed-in label has been removed from the garment.) Slowly he replaces the coat, then takes down another garment, goes through the same performance. He whistles very softly between his teeth, stands a moment with a puzzled expression on his face, replaces the garment. Exits closet. Light goes out.

QUICK DISSOLVE TO

36    LOBBY OUTSIDE PENTHOUSE

As elevator comes up. Killaine exits elevator, crosses, presses buzzer beside Brandon's door. Brandon opens it, Killaine nods to him, passes him on the way in.

37    INTERIOR. PENTHOUSE LIVING ROOM

As Killaine enters, stops, looking around.

> KILLAINE
> I'm sorry to have kept you waiting. Mrs. West, Mr. Clarendon.
> *(he turns to Betty)*
> Miss Mayfield. There's not much I can do tonight. But there is one thing.
> *(he moves across to Clarendon,*
> *takes gun and handkerchief out of his pocket and holds*
> *it so only Clarendon can see it)*
> Mr. Clarendon, have you ever seen this before?

> CLARENDON
> *(looking down at the gun)*
> I'm sorry, Inspector, I don't know much about—

> KILLAINE
> *(sharply)*
> Recently, then.

> CLARENDON
> *(slowly)*
> No. Not recently. I'm sure of that.

> KILLAINE
> Thank you.

He moves to Margo, holds gun in front of her.

57

KILLAINE

Mrs. West?

Margo's eyes go down very slowly. She stares at the gun for a long moment before speaking.

MARGO
*(in a choked voice)*
I never saw it before.

KILLAINE

Positive?

Margo lifts her face to him and nods.

KILLAINE

Thank you.

He moves on to Brandon, shows him the gun.

KILLAINE

How about you, Brandon?

BRANDON

Yes, I've seen it before.

Margo reacts sharply. Killaine catches the reaction with the corner of his eye, but appears not to pay any attention. Brandon obviously does see the reaction. Killaine turns back to Brandon.

KILLAINE

Where?

BRANDON

On Miss Mayfield's balcony—beside the chaise. I picked it up. Don't ask me why. I ought to know better.

KILLAINE

Quite sure you had no motive?
*(Killaine glances sidewise at Betty)*

BRANDON

Could be.


KILLAINE

I rather thought so. And before that, had you ever
seen the gun?


BRANDON

No.

Margo is seen to react with great relief which she tries to
conceal. Killaine gives her another quick sidelong look.
Brandon has continued to watch her.


KILLAINE
*(to Brandon)*
It was lying where on the balcony?


BRANDON

Near his right hand. About a foot away. Perhaps
more. Good heavens, one doesn't use a tape
measure.


KILLAINE

*We* do—when we get a chance.

Killaine turns so that he faces Margo and Clarendon.


KILLAINE

I needn't keep you any longer, Mr. Clarendon.


CLARENDON
*(standing up)*
Thank you. It *is* rather late—and I'm not young
anymore. Good night.


MARGO

What about me?


KILLAINE

Not quite yet.

He crosses and opens door. Clarendon goes out. Killaine
shuts door, goes to Margo.

KILLAINE

You knew Mitchell pretty well, didn't you, Mrs. West?

MARGO

I was in love with him—which shows you the quality of my brains.
*(bursting out—looking at Betty)*
Why don't you ask *her* about the gun?

KILLAINE

I shall. From your knowledge of Mitchell, would you say he would be likely to commit suicide?

MARGO

Anybody could commit suicide, if he felt low enough. I've felt like it myself.

KILLAINE

Then why not give Miss Mayfield the benefit of the doubt?

MARGO

I'd be delighted to—any time you can show me the doubt. I'll wrap it up in tissue paper and put Christmas seals on it for her.

KILLAINE

Thank you very much, Mrs. West.

Margo flounces to door, jerks it open before anybody can get there to hold it for her, and goes out, banging the door after her.

BRANDON

How about a cup of coffee?

KILLAINE

No thanks. I had some. How would you like to take a walk for, say, half an hour.

Brandon glances at Betty, then back at Killaine. Shrugs.

BRANDON

All right.

He crosses, gets hat and coat, goes to door and out. Killaine turns to Betty.

KILLAINE

Mrs. West is a very emotional woman.

BETTY

I don't know her—or particularly want to.

KILLAINE

You probably know the type. You find them in hotels and resorts all over the world. They always have clothes, and money, and usually have had three or four husbands. They dress and enamel themselves with great care. They worry a great deal about those little lines at the corner of the eyes—and they demonstrate their incompetence at the art of living by getting mixed up with people like Larry Mitchell.
*(pause)*
Tell me about yourself, Miss Mayfield.

BETTY

I was born in New York City. I grew up. And here I am.

KILLAINE

I'll have to know a little more than that.

BETTY

I'm sorry, that's all there is.

KILLAINE

Miss Mayfield, the humor of the situation escapes me. Within 12 hours I shall know officially whether Mitchell was murdered. Privately, I'm quite sure of it now. It happened in your room, and you came to Vancouver with him—at any rate, he made your hotel reservation—and you arrived together. Here in this room he behaved very nastily to you, and

you said something to him which might be taken as a threat. A few hours later he was found dead on your balcony. Would it be too much to suggest that all these circumstances taken together are a little suspicious?
(Betty doesn't answer)
Please answer my question.

                    BETTY
You didn't ask a question. You made a speech.

                  KILLAINE
That's an evasion and you know it.

                    BETTY
        Is it?

Their eyes meet in a long stare.

38    INTERIOR. MARGO'S LIVING ROOM IN DARKNESS

There is some moonlight. In foreground, the back of a man seated in a chair. Door opens, Margo is silhouetted against corridor light. She switches light on, shuts door, turns, and reacts violently. Clarendon is sitting in chair with his cane between his knees. CAMERA PANS her over to Clarendon.

                    MARGO
                  (tensely)
What are you doing here?

                  CLARENDON
I don't think you locked your door.

                    MARGO
What do you want?

                  CLARENDON
See how easy it is? Perhaps Miss Mayfield left her door unlocked. Or if she didn't, there's a passkey on every floor in the linen room. The head porter has a passkey. The bell captain has a passkey. The hotel's full of passkeys.

MARGO
*(shaken)*

Passkey?

CLARENDON

Or—since one is a well-known and respected guest—one could go to the desk in the lobby and say, "Miss Mayfield seems to have lost her room key—have you another?" They always have another.

MARGO

Don't be a fool. I loved him. He wasn't worth it, but I loved him.

CLARENDON

And now that he's safe from all other women, you can go on loving him.

MARGO

You nasty, sardonic—

CLARENDON

Sardonic, if you will, my dear. But not nasty. You lied about the gun.

Margo reacts, shocked. Clarendon gets slowly to his feet.

CLARENDON

I'm a very observant man. You had something in your bag this afternoon. Something that caused you to hold it in a peculiar way. Something that made a peculiar sound when you put it down on the bar. You went out with Mitchell. None of us ever saw him again.

MARGO
*(desperately)*

That isn't enough.

CLARENDON

I saw your face this evening when the detective showed you the gun. You lied. It was obvious.

MARGO

He saw my face, too.

CLARENDON

So he did—but he hasn't told you what he saw. I have.

MARGO

They'll arrest that girl. Everything points to her.

CLARENDON

Convenient, isn't it?

He starts towards door.

MARGO

One of these days, you're going to wake up in the middle of the night and find that you've cut your throat.

CLARENDON
*(turning)*
How clumsy. I'd never forgive myself. Good night, my dear.

MARGO

You could have got in that room, just as you got in here. How do I know you didn't kill Larry?

Clarendon reacts. There is something that might be fear in his face.

CLARENDON

With what motive?

MARGO

Nastiness. You're nasty with words. Why wouldn't you be nasty with deeds once in a while? You hated him—and I know why.

CLARENDON

He was very easy to hate. If you'll look in your mirror, when you are in a better temper—you'll know why.

64

(*Margo just stares at him*)
Very silly of me, isn't it? I'm not as well-off as I was
once—and I'm used to my little comforts.

He exits. Margo looks after him, thunderstruck.

39     EXTERIOR. BRANDON'S PENTHOUSE TERRACE

Killaine is standing at wall, looking out over view. He is
smoking. He points up with cigarette.

KILLAINE
That star up there is Alphard. "The lonely," they
call him. I wonder why he's lonely. Perhaps he's a
policeman—a celestial policeman.

CAMERA PULLS BACK to include Betty, who is staring at
him. He turns slowly.

KILLAINE
Well, that's not getting us anywhere. You won't tell
me who you are, or give any account of yourself.
You won't even give me your address in the
United States. Why? Unhappy marriage?

BETTY
Who told you I was married?

KILLAINE
There's the clear mark of a wedding ring on your
finger.

She turns, walks abruptly away, then back into the living
room. Killaine follows.

40     INTERIOR OF LIVING ROOM

as Killaine enters. Betty is already inside. She sits down.

BETTY
I want a cigarette.

KILLAINE
The room's full of cigarettes. But of course one
would have to be handed to you.

65

He goes to her, takes out silver case, and opens it. She takes one, he takes one, is about to return the case to his pocket, when:

BETTY

Let me see that.

He holds case out to her. There is an inlaid design on it.

BETTY

Your family coat of arms, Mr. Killaine?

KILLAINE
(crossly)
Regimental. Seaforth Highlanders.

BETTY

Oh. Are you Scotch?

KILLAINE

The Canadian Seaforths. You don't have to be Scotch to belong to them.

BETTY

I'm sorry.

KILLAINE

Stop saying you're sorry. I want information, not regrets.

BETTY

Would you be satisfied if I said I shot him?

Killaine jerks the wrapped gun out of his pocket and thrusts it in front of her.

KILLAINE

With this?

BETTY

Yes.

66

KILLAINE

Where'd you get it?

BETTY

A graduation present.

Killaine puts the gun back in his pocket.

KILLAINE

That's a rather inferior grade of humor. But since
you're being so frank, would you mind telling me
why all the labels have been removed from your
clothes?

Betty is jarred. She doesn't answer.

KILLAINE

An unhappy marriage hardly seems a sufficient
reason for that.

BETTY

Why don't you arrest me and be done with it.

KILLAINE

I probably shall—after I've tortured you a little
more.

SOUND OF ROOM DOOR OPENING OFF. Killaine looks
towards it. Brandon comes in and shuts door, throws hat and
coat to one side.

BRANDON

How are you two getting along?

KILLAINE

Delightfully. Every time Miss Mayfield says something, I know less than I knew before.
                    (pause)
Well, I may as well knock off for tonight.
                    (turns to Betty)
Goodnight, Miss Mayfield. Do let me thank you
for your cooperation.

BETTY

There's one thing I may as well tell you. You'll find it out anyhow. I tried to run away—when I found him out there on the balcony. There wasn't any plane.

BRANDON

You didn't have to tell him that.

KILLAINE
(dryly)

Why not?
(he picks up his trench coat
and starts to put it on)
Especially as I already knew it.

He goes out. They watch him leave. As the door closes, Brandon turns to Betty.

BRANDON

Bad?

BETTY

Bad enough.

BRANDON

He could hardly help suspecting you.

BETTY

That's putting it very mildly.

She walks across to French doors and stands looking out.

BETTY
(over her shoulder)

What time is it?

BRANDON
(looking at watch)

Quarter after one. Why?

BETTY

There's a lot of night left to live through.

68

BRANDON

So there is. You don't want to go to bed. I don't
want to go to bed. Let's go somewhere and hear
music—have something to drink—something to
eat—even dance.

BETTY

Dance? Tonight?

BRANDON

Let's not pretend Mitchell meant anything to either
of us.

BETTY

Certainly not to me.

BRANDON

Just who are you, anyway?

BETTY

You, too?
*(pause)*
My name is Betty Mayfield. I was born, and I am
here. Message ends. That's what I told him. He
didn't like it.

BRANDON

I'm different. I like it fine.

DISSOLVE TO

41    INTERIOR OF LOBBY—NIGHT—DESK AND ELEVATOR
BANK

Killaine is standing at the desk, holding a registration card in
his hand. A clerk is across the desk from him.

KILLAINE

Nice writing—but no information.
*(he hands card to clerk)*
I didn't expect any.

Elevator comes down, doors open. Betty and Brandon come
out. Killaine turns, sees them. Brandon crosses to Killaine.

BRANDON

Miss Mayfield would like a little fresh air. Any
objections?
*(Killaine shakes his head)*
In case you want to have us followed—

KILLAINE
*(curtly)*

I don't.

BRANDON

Well—good night.

Killaine looks past him at Betty. Their eyes meet. Killaine
turns away quickly. Brandon rejoins Betty and they start out
of scene.

42  TRUCKING SHOT—BRANDON AND BETTY WALKING

Lobby is very empty. A short, thick-set man is trimming a
cigar in a chair. They pass in front of him. He looks up, stares
hard at Betty. Betty meets his glance, looks away quickly. She
and Brandon go on, CAMERA STOPS, HOLDS ON SEATED
MAN. He looks after them, puts away his pocket knife, lights
cigar leisurely, stands up, goes after them.

DISSOLVE TO

43  EXTERIOR OF STREET—WATERFRONT

Mooring slips on one side, below a sea wall. On the other
side, a row of nondescript buildings, a few of which have
electric signs, one of them an old-fashioned winking electric
sign. It is a run-down neighborhood and tough. A couple of
merchant marine sailors lurch along street, drunk. Brandon's
convertible enters shot, pulls over to curb in front of blinking
sign.

44  CLOSER SHOT

Sign is now seen to be "CHARLIE'S" but the "R" is half out,
dead bulbs. Car stops, Brandon and Betty get out.

45  CLOSE SHOT—BRANDON AND BETTY ON SIDEWALK IN
FRONT OF CHARLIE'S

Betty is shivering.

BRANDON

Cold?


BETTY

Is this the best you can do?


BRANDON

At this time of night. It's not as bad as it looks.

A little reluctantly, she crosses sidewalk with him, they go into swinging double doors. As the doors open, sounds of very bad dance music are heard. Doors swing shut again. CAMERA PULLS BACK AND PANS SLOWLY ALONG STREET, as the nondescript little car with dim lights comes up to curb and stops some way behind Brandon's convertible. Lights go out, and the short, thick-set man from lobby of hotel gets out of car, walks along to Brandon's car, leans in, pokes a small pencil flash at the registration on the steering post, takes out a notebook, makes a note in it, puts notebook and flash away, crosses to swinging doors, starts in.

46    INTERIOR OF CHARLIE'S UPSTAIRS DINE AND DANCE ROOM

The decor is strictly Gashouse Gothic. There are booths like horse stalls, also round scarred tables and hard chairs. The dance band on plain wooden platform, composed of five old-young men, plays moodily and contemptuously. There isn't a thing in the joint that could be damaged by being dropped out of a third-story window. At one table sits a Navy sailor across from a blowsy girl. There is an empty glass in front of him. He sits very straight, vacant-eyed, stupid drunk. A chunky grim-looking character in a dinner jacket comes by table, pauses to glance at sailor, makes signal to girl, who nods. Chunky character goes on, CAMERA PANS him across to booth in which Brandon and Betty have just sat down. The man in dinner jacket is Magruder. He owns the joint.


MAGRUDER

Nice to see you, Mr. Brandon—and the lady. What'll you take?


BRANDON
(glancing at Betty)

Scotch?

71

*(Betty nods lifelessly; to Magruder)*
Scotch. The kind you buy, Magruder, not the kind
you make.

MAGRUDER
Only the best for you, Mr. Brandon.

He signals a waiter, goes out of shot. Band starts to play. Betty
looks out of booth.

47     ANOTHER ANGLE—WHAT SHE SEES

Three couples start to lumber around the small dance floor.
The air is heavy with smoke. The soused sailor and blowsy
girl come dancing into foreground. Sailor is dancing with all
the grace of a rhinoceros.

BLOWSY GIRL
What you need is a drink, big boy.

SAILOR
*(suddenly pushing her away)*
Aw, go blow your nose.

He starts back to table. Girl shrugs resignedly, goes after him.

48     BRANDON AND BETTY

She is staring horrified at this.

BETTY
Why did you bring me to such a place?

BRANDON
*(casually)*
There isn't anywhere else.

Waiter comes up and serves drinks. Brandon tastes it to make
sure he gets what he orders, nods his head. Betty seizes glass
almost convulsively and takes a long swallow.

BRANDON
Want to dance?

72

BETTY

Dance? Here?

BRANDON

Why not?

BETTY
*(staring at him)*
They know you here—know your name.

BRANDON

I know everybody. I don't look at half of life, just
the nice half, I look at all of it.

Betty finishes off her drink, then in a reckless, half-wild voice,

BETTY
All right, then, let's dance.

They get up out of booth and are about to start dancing when
Betty's gaze becomes fixed on something across the room.

49     WHAT SHE SEES

Thick-set man from lobby is sitting alone at a table with a
bottle of beer in front of him. He is staring over at Betty and
Brandon.

50     BACK TO BETTY AND BRANDON

BETTY
That man over there. He was in the hotel lobby.

BRANDON
*(he looks across)*
I didn't notice him.

BETTY
We walked right past him. He's following us.

BRANDON
Killaine's not that sort of a guy. He said no—he
meant no.

                    BETTY
        Then he's not a police detective.

                    BRANDON
        Couldn't be.

                    BETTY
        Then he's—
                *(she breaks off, stares rigidly)*

Brandon looks at her curiously, not getting it. Betty swallows,
then gets her voice.

                    BETTY
        Take me out of here, please. Right away.
                *(Brandon just keeps looking at her)*
        If you don't, I'll go alone.

Brandon reaches for her coat, puts it around her, throws
some money on the table. They start across room. Brandon
deliberately steers her past the thick-set man, who is pouring
himself a glass of beer. He doesn't even look up. Brandon and
Betty reach the top of the stairs. Brandon looks back.

                    BRANDON
        Quite sure you saw him in the hotel lobby?

                    BETTY
        Absolutely sure.

                    BRANDON
                *(his eyes narrow a little)*
        We'll find out.

He turns, takes Betty's arm, they start down stairs, CAMERA
PANS OVER TO MAN. He is now looking after them with a
half smile on his face. He lifts his glass of beer in salute,
drinks it down, stands up.

51    FOOT OF STAIRS JUST INSIDE SWINGING DOORS

It is pretty dark. It is not a solid stairway, there is a space
behind it. Brandon notes this.

                    BRANDON
        You go out and get in the car.

74

Betty hesitates, then starts out. Brandon looks back upstairs. SOUND OF DESCENDING STEPS OVER SHOT. Brandon goes quickly around stairway almost out of sight. Thick-set man comes down stairs. He is now trimming another cigar. As he reaches the bottom of stairs, he stops, takes out a match, and is about to strike it when Brandon steps out. The man looks at him unemotionally, cigar and match in midair.

> BRANDON
> The light's bad in here, but I seem to remember the face. What was the name?

Man smiles, doesn't answer.

> BRANDON
> All right, let's see the buzzer.

> MAN
> What's a buzzer?

> BRANDON
> So you're not a cop.

> MAN
> Me a cop? What made you think that, Mr. Brandon?

> BRANDON
> Who told you my name?

> MAN
> I've got good ears.

Brandon steps up close to him, grabs the lapels of his coat, and twists a little.

> BRANDON
> (tightly)
> How are your teeth getting along?

> MAN
> (smiling)
> The new ones are fine. The last set I had gave me all kinds of trouble.

He looks down at Brandon's hand, holding the lapels of his coat.

                          MAN
          What's this in favor of?

                        BRANDON
          I don't like to be tailed. The lady I'm with doesn't
          like to be stared at. To put the matter in a couple of
          nutshells, I don't like you.

Still smiling, the man brings his knee up hard. Brandon reels away from him, groaning, doubles up against the wall.

                          MAN
          You wanta get tough, Mr. Brandon, you gotta
          know the technique. Next time, turn a little side-
          ways, get your hip in the way. See what I mean?
          Good night.

He goes out through the double doors. CAMERA STAYS ON BRANDON. He straightens up slowly, gets out handkerchief, mops his forehead. He has been hurt pretty badly. After a while, he stiffens himself by main force, walks to door, pushes it open, starts out.

52    EXTERIOR OF STREET AS BRANDON COMES UP

He stands, breathing hard, looking off.

53    WHAT HE SEES

Thick-set man is getting into his little car. He starts it up, turns the lights on, turns and goes out of shot.

54    BACK TO BRANDON

He crosses sidewalk slowly to his convertible. Betty is waiting in it. Without a word, Brandon goes around, gets in behind wheel. He sits there with his hands on the wheel, taking deep breaths.

                         BETTY
                        (urgently)
          Who is he?

76

Brandon turns his head slowly to look at her. He speaks a little thickly, still in pain.

                    BRANDON
He's a fellow with a very hard knee, and he knows how to use it.

                    BETTY
You don't know who he is?

                    BRANDON
He's not a cop. A cop wouldn't have kneed me.

                    BETTY
                    (slowly)
He was following us—but he's not a policeman.

                    BRANDON
Us?

                    BETTY
All right—following me.

                    BRANDON
Why?

                    BETTY
No matter. There's nothing I can do about it.

                    BRANDON
Anything I can do about it?

                    BETTY
Take me home—and forget you ever saw me. That's a silly remark, isn't it?

                    BRANDON
Try not talking.

He puts an arm around her and pulls her close to him as if to kiss her.

                    BRANDON
It still doesn't matter if I kiss you?

                    BETTY
Nothing matters.

                    BRANDON
No use waiting, then.

He kisses her on the mouth, hard. She doesn't resist and she doesn't respond. He pulls his head away.

                    BRANDON
That's the second round I've lost tonight.
                  *(he moves and winces)*
That fellow hurt me.

                    BETTY
So have I.

                    BRANDON
From you, I like it.

He starts the car. It goes off down the street.

FADE IN

55    INTERIOR OF HOTEL LOBBY—DAY

A very wide shot, showing desk, elevator bank, guests reading morning papers in chairs. In background the dining room entrance through which can be seen part of the dining room, with waiters moving back and forth, etc. It is breakfast time. Betty appears in dining room entrance, coming out.

56    CLOSE SHOT—BETTY

CAMERA PANS with her as she moves across lobby to desk. Room clerk is checking in several new arrivals. Luggage, bellboys, etc. Betty moves along the desk to far end, stands waiting. Hotel manager comes up to her. He pretends not to know her.

                    MANAGER
Good morning. Can I do something for you?

BETTY

I'm Miss Mayfield. Is Mr. Campbell here?

MANAGER

I'm Mr. Campbell, Miss Mayfield.
(slight pause)
Purely as a matter of routine, I want to ask you the
name of your bank.

BETTY

Bank?

MANAGER

(very smoothly)
Merely for our records, Miss Mayfield. It's usual
for the guests who come here for the first time.

BETTY

(opening her bag)
I'm carrying quite a large sum in Travellers'
Checks. How much of a deposit would you like?

CAMPBELL

I wouldn't dream of questioning your credit.
Purely a matter of routine, for the hotel records.
Just the name of your bank—

He breaks off, glances over to one side.

57      CLOSE REVERSE SHOT—BETTY

She notices the glance and turns her head, looks off, in the
same direction, reacts, looks back at Campbell.

BETTY

(sharply, with emphasis)
The *hotel* records, Mr. Campbell?

58      TWO SHOT—CAMPBELL AND BETTY

CAMPBELL

(brightly)
I'm afraid I've been clumsy. Please overlook it,
Miss Mayfield.

79

With a quick nod, Betty turns away. CAMERA PANS her over to extreme end of desk. Killaine stands there idly, with an elbow on the desk. Betty comes up to him. She is angry.

BETTY
Good morning, Mr. Killaine. I'm sorry I can't give you the name of my bank—because I have no bank at the moment.
*(pause)*
That was a pretty crude trick.

KILLAINE
They're all crude, when they don't work. Had breakfast?
*(she nods)*
Care for a stroll outside? Beautiful morning. The air is like wine, the sky is a deep blue.

BETTY
*(contemptuously)*
Deep blue? I'd call it gray-blue.

KILLAINE
You must come from pretty far South.
*(she bites her lip)*
Florida?

BETTY
I've never been to Florida.

Killaine smiles and moves away from desk, and she falls in beside him.

QUICK DISSOLVE TO

59    CLOSE SHOT—AN OFFICE DOOR

Metal lettering on it reads CLARK BRANDON ENTER-PRISES. Below that, to one side, ENTER.

60    INTERIOR. BRANDON'S OFFICE RECEPTION ROOM

A middle-aged secretary is at a desk. A man sitting over to one side, reading a newspaper. He is short, thick-set, wears very heavy glasses. (These are phony glasses—they just look

heavy—there is a clear spot in the middle.) DOOR OPENS
OFF. Brandon enters shot, goes across to desk.

> SECRETARY
> Good morning, Mr. Brandon.

> BRANDON
> Morning. Any calls?

> SECRETARY
> Mr. Reed would like you to call him.

> BRANDON
> All right. Get him.

> SECRETARY
> *(looking off)*
> And there's a Mr. Goble to see you. Says his
> business is personal.

> BRANDON
> Who's Goble?

CAMERA PANS OVER TO MAN with glasses. He puts his
newspaper away, stands up, crosses to Brandon, CAMERA
PANNING HIM BACK.

> MAN
> I'm Goble.

Brandon looks at him. Nothing in his face shows recognition.

> GOBLE
> I'd like a few words with you, in private.

> BRANDON
> I'm not interested in blind dates.

Goble takes his glasses off, puts them away, and stares at
Brandon, who reacts just enough to show he has recognized
Goble. During this, secretary has dialed.

81

SECRETARY
*(into phone)*
Mr. Reed, please, for Mr. Brandon.
*(pause)*
Very well. Have him call. Mr. Brandon is in his
office now.
*(she hangs up)*
Mr. Reed stepped out, Mr. Brandon.

Brandon nods without turning.

BRANDON
*(to Goble)*
This way.

He crosses to door, opens it, goes in, leaving Goble to follow.

61    INTERIOR OF BRANDON'S PRIVATE OFFICE

Brandon rounds desk, takes off hat, stands looking down at
some letters on his desk. DOOR CLOSES BEHIND Goble,
who has entered. Goble crosses calmly to chair, sits down.
Brandon gets a cigarette out and lights it with desk lighter,
without offering Goble one, and blows a little smoke.

BRANDON
All right. Talk it up.

Goble gets a card out of a wallet, hands it across.

BRANDON
*(reading)*
Martin Goble. Insurance Adjuster.

He drops card on desk, smiles.

BRANDON
Nice friendly approach you've got, Goble. I could
hardly walk when I got out of bed this morning.

GOBLE
You asked for it.

BRANDON
I'm still asking. What do you want?

82

GOBLE

I'm not sure I want anything from you. You might want something from me.

BRANDON

Name it.

GOBLE

Information—protection—you might even want to hire me to go home and listen to the radio. That's the funny part of my business—once in a while, I get hired not to work.
(*pause*)
Nice girl you were with last night. Known her long?

Brandon picks the card off the desk, tosses it into waste paper basket.

BRANDON

Private eye?

GOBLE

You guessed it. The card's a phony. I got plenty of 'em. Different names, different jobs. I work out of San Francisco. Go anywhere, do anything. All it takes is the folding.

BRANDON

What are your rates?

GOBLE

$40 a day and expenses. Expenses run pretty high on a case like this. I'm a long way from home. I don't have a B.C. license. I'd need about $500 for a retainer.

BRANDON

What have you got on Miss Mayfield?

GOBLE

Mayfield? Oh, that girl you were with last night. You haven't hired me yet, Mr. Brandon.

Brandon moves quickly around desk, grabs Goble, and jerks him to his feet.

                    BRANDON
                 *(with cold savagery)*
That's a nice hard knee you've got, Goble. How'd you like to trade it for a broken neck?

                    GOBLE
                    *(calmly)*
Quit trying to scare me, Brandon, I'm neurotic.

                    BRANDON
I don't know whether to knock your teeth down your throat—or call the police—or just give you twenty bucks to go out and buy yourself a clean nose.

Brandon hurls him away. Goble staggers back, without losing his balance. He smiles. Brandon stares at him savagely for a moment, then goes back around his desk and sits down.

                    GOBLE
You hurt my feelings. I ought to raise the price to a thousand.

                    BRANDON
If I call the police, your price will go down to a minus sign.

                    GOBLE
Bluff. You've waited too long.

                    BRANDON
For five hundred, what do I get?

                    GOBLE
I go home and paint the kitchen.

                    BRANDON
For two hundred?

                    GOBLE
I stick around and wait for the five hundred.

                          BRANDON
You mentioned information.

                          GOBLE
Sorry. Another client paid for that. You can hire me
not to use it.

                          BRANDON
A thousand.

                          GOBLE
                    *(hesitates—then)*
Got it on you?

                          BRANDON
Got the information on you?

                          GOBLE
Get it in half an hour.

Brandon takes out his wallet, takes some bills out of it,
throws them across the desk.

                          BRANDON
There's two hundred. I'll meet you in an hour—
where we met last night.

                          GOBLE
Why not here?

                          BRANDON
I don't like your perfume in my office. Make it
somewhere else, if you don't like Charlie's.

                          GOBLE
Charlie's suits me fine. I don't scare.

He reaches for the money, stands up and puts it in his pocket.

                          GOBLE
You pay the check, you pick the joint. See you.

He exits scene.

                            85

62    A WALL AT THE FOOT OF THE HOTEL GARDENS

BETTY AND KILLAINE are leaning on it, looking out over
Puget Sound.

> KILLAINE
> Down below's Stanley Park. On the other side of
> the trees, there's a beach. You can't see it.
> *(points over to left)*
> Steveston's over there. Coast Guard station.
> *(points to right)*
> There's the Yacht Club, and beyond it, the docks.
> Then over on the other side of the inlet, there's
> Grouse Mountain. It's about 4000 feet high. There's
> a restaurant on top of it. Very nice restaurant.
> *(he turns to Betty)*
> I'm sorry we couldn't have met in pleasanter
> circumstances, Miss Mayfield.

> BETTY
> We wouldn't have met at all.

> KILLAINE
> True. I was a bit irritable last night. I apologize.

> BETTY
> You were a Galahad, compared to some cops I've
> known.

> KILLAINE
> *(pouncing—but very quietly)*
> You've had dealings with the police before?

> BETTY
> Who hasn't—one way or another?

> KILLAINE
> But not in the investigation of a major crime, I
> hope.

> BETTY
> Is it a crime?

KILLAINE

We're 98 per cent certain Mitchell was murdered.
There are a lot of reasons.
*(pause)*
Was he very drunk when you last saw him?

BETTY

You were there when I last saw him.

KILLAINE

I'd like to believe that. It's not too easy.

Betty says nothing. Killaine looks away again.

KILLAINE

I've been talking to the Immigration Inspector who
passed you across the border. He was a little
suspicious of you. Mayfield isn't really your name,
is it?
*(Betty looks straight ahead, doesn't answer)*
I'll find out, you know. Perhaps not today—
perhaps not tomorrow. But in the end, I'll find out.

BETTY

The police always do, don't they?

KILLAINE

You've had an experience that you don't want to
talk about. An unhappy marriage, for example.
*(Betty turns away quickly)*
I wouldn't make you talk about it. My job is the
death of Larry Mitchell. Why can't you give me
your confidence?

BETTY

You—or the Vancouver Police Department?

KILLAINE

We try to be decent.

BETTY

You're a police officer. A very nice one—but you
have a job to do. I'm a girl who's in a jam, and it's

your job to keep me there. Don't go considerate on me. I might start to bawl.

Their eyes meet in a long look.

                    KILLAINE
You won't tell me who you are. You won't even give me a chance to help you.

                    BETTY
Nobody can help me. You, least of all.

                    KILLAINE
                    (suddenly)
If I understand what you mean by that.

                    BETTY
You understand perfectly.

                    KILLAINE
Then there isn't much I can do, is there?

                    BETTY
There isn't anything you can do.

He moves towards her, then turns abruptly and goes.

WIPE TO

63    INTERIOR. CHARLIE'S PLACE—DAY

Chairs are piled up on the tables. A man with a mop is going over the floor. STEPS ARE HEARD. Goble, the private eye, comes into the shot slowly. His eyes are very wary. He has a hand in his pocket.

                    GOBLE
I came here to see Mr. Brandon.

                    MAN WITH MOP
Who?

                    GOBLE
Brandon. I was to meet him here.

MAN

O.K. Ask the boss.

He jerks his thumb backwards, and Goble moves off in that direction.

64    BACK OF THE ROOM—DOOR OPENING INTO SMALL DARK HALL

CAMERA FOLLOWS GOBLE through it. He stands a moment, looking along the hallway, listening. There is no sound at all. He reaches a door. CAMERA PANS AROUND to show small plate on the door with the word MANAGER. Goble listens again, takes the gun out of his pocket, looks at it, puts it back, keeping his hand on it, opens the door, and starts in.

65    INTERIOR—MANAGER'S OFFICE AT CHARLIE'S

It is what you would expect. Magruder is at a desk doing some bookkeeping work. He looks up indifferently as Goble ENTERS.

GOBLE

I'm looking for Mr. Brandon.

MAGRUDER

The joint's not open, Mac. Who's Brandon?

Goble comes up to the desk.

GOBLE

I have an appointment with him, right here, right now.

MAGRUDER

Go live in a tent.

GOBLE

It'll be a tough dollar when guys like you learn the alphabet.

MAGRUDER
(grinning)

Talk English. How do I know you're you?

89

Goble reaches a hand into his pocket, throws a card on the desk. Magruder picks it up, reads it.

> MAGRUDER
>
> Mr. Brandon couldn't be here. He might have left something for you. What would it look like?

> GOBLE
>
> One of those nice long manila envelopes—sealed. Not too fat—not too thin.

> MAGRUDER
>
> What do I get for it?

> GOBLE
>
> You get its brother.

> MAGRUDER
>
> Sounds like a fair swap. Let's take a look.

He jerks open the drawer of his desk. Goble stiffens, his hand on the gun. Magruder takes out a long sealed envelope, throws it on the desk.

> MAGRUDER
>
> I need a receipt. Sign your name across the flap.

> GOBLE
>
> Open it up and count it.

> MAGRUDER
>
> When you sign for it, *you* count it. It's *your* dough.

He picks up a desk pen, holds it out. Goble hesitates, then takes his right hand holding the gun out of his pocket, lays the gun down on the desk beside the envelope. He takes the pen, leans down to write. At that instant, Magruder lunges up swiftly, grabs Goble's right wrist with his left hand and jerks him forward, hard. Goble tries to reach the gun with his left hand. Magruder grabs an old-fashioned round ebony ruler up off the desk and smacks Goble hard on the head with it twice. Goble sprawls across the desk, limp. Magruder takes the gun, puts it in his pocket, picks up the envelope, tears it open, and shakes out the money, counts it.

MAGRUDER
Eight hundred bucks. Ice cream for dinner.

Magruder picks the gun up, balances it on his hand. MOVE IN ON THE GUN. It is a .32 caliber revolver, with part of the barrel sawed off to make it a belly gun. It has no front sight. Magruder stares down at it. PULL AWAY as he turns, pulls open desk drawer, puts gun in it, shuts drawer. He rounds the desk, reaches inside Goble's pocket, pulls out a thick manila envelope, stands looking down at it, speculating, tries the flap to see if it will come loose. MOVE IN TO SHOW THERE IS NO WRITING ON THE ENVELOPE. He picks up the envelope which contained the money. It is also manila and about the same size. With a quick decision, Magruder tears open GOBLE'S ENVELOPE, draws out a sheaf of blank paper. Magruder whistles lightly between his teeth, turns his head to stare at Goble who is still limp, sprawled across the desk.

MAGRUDER
(softly)
You had it coming, didn't you, baby?
(reaches across, shakes Goble's shoulder)
Come on. You're not that sick.

Goble does not respond. Magruder pulls his head and shoulders up off the desk. The head sags to one side. Magruder presses a thumb against one of Goble's eyeballs. No reaction. Magruder bends close, stares, and is suddenly stiff with fear.

MAGRUDER
(hoarsely)
Don't tell me you had a glass head, baby. Oh no—
not in your business. How could you live so long?

He lets go of Goble who sways sideways in the chair, his head hanging like that of a broken doll. As Magruder stares down at him, with very much the sort of frozen horror as we saw on Betty's face when she found Mitchell's body on the balcony.

91

66     INTERIOR—KILLAINE'S OFFICE AT HEADQUARTERS

Small bare room, empty. Door opens. Sergeant Gore ushers Margo in through a side door.

GORE
Sit down, Mrs. West. Inspector Killaine will be along in a minute.

MARGO
Thank you.

Gore exits. She sits down in a hard wooden chair by Killaine's desk. She is nervous, lights cigarette, looks at her watch, gets up suddenly as if to leave before Killaine gets back, then shrugs and sits down again. Door opens and Killaine enters, glances at Margo, goes behind his desk, sits down with his hat on, presses dictagraph key.

KILLAINE
(into dictagraph)
Killaine here. I want a radio contact to work with Handley. A motorcycle officer will do.

VOICE FROM DICTAGRAPH
Right away, Inspector.

Killaine disconnects, turns to face Margo, removing his hat.

KILLAINE
Remembered that time, didn't I? Good morning, Mrs. West. Does your visit here mean you've changed your mind?

MARGO
(startled)
How did you know?
(Killaine smiles slightly, doesn't answer)
Clarendon?
(Killaine still doesn't answer)
You cops never tell anybody anything, do you?

KILLAINE

Other people always know so much more than we
know—so much more than they're willing to tell
us.

MARGO

It was Clarendon, then. He knew I had the gun in
my bag.
(Killaine just stares)
You couldn't possibly have traced it this soon—not
possibly.

KILLAINE
(dryly)
Of course not. Thanks for telling me. I haven't
seen Mr. Clarendon.

MARGO

I *am* a fool.

KILLAINE

That depends upon your motive. You were in love
with Mitchell, weren't you?

MARGO

Yes—and he's already becoming vague to me.
Funny! Last night I was furiously jealous. Jealous
of what? I put that gun in my bag deliberately.
Who was I going to kill with it? A girl I didn't even
know? A man I knew to be a thief and a forger? A
half-man? A gigolo? It's already ludicrous. Love!
What a comedy!

KILLAINE

You didn't play it for laughs last night.

MARGO

Did you ever have a serious operation?

KILLAINE

Mortar shells are not funny, either.

MARGO

At first, it doesn't hurt at all. That's shock. Then it hurts terribly—you wouldn't believe such pain could exist—and six months later you can't remember what it felt like.
*(pause)*
It hasn't taken six months this time. It hasn't even taken twenty-four hours. Is that a beastly thing to say?

KILLAINE

Not if it clears the air.

MARGO

It does. May I go now?
*(she stands up)*

KILLAINE

I'll investigate Mr. Clarendon's financial position—

MARGO

I don't understand.

KILLAINE

Perhaps a rich widow would have solved all his problems.

MARGO

Now *you're* being beastly.

KILLAINE

Sure. You didn't come here in person just to tell me about the gun. You wanted me to be looking across the desk at you while you talked about Mitchell.
*(he pauses; Margo nods—admiration in her eyes)*
If I believed you, it would be psychologically impossible for you to have killed him last night.

MARGO

And if you didn't believe me?

KILLAINE

You would still have planted the information that Clarendon knew about the gun—and not as an accusation, but in the process of defending yourself by making a confession. Very neat. Good morning, Mrs. West.

Her expression changes. She gives him an icy stare, and goes out quickly. Dictagraph BUZZES. He depresses key.

KILLAINE
*(into speaker)*
Killaine here.

SUPT. McKECHNIE'S VOICE
*(Scotch accent)*
Come into my office, please, Killaine.

KILLAINE
Right away, sir.

He releases key, starts out.

67 INTERIOR OF CORRIDOR

As Killaine comes out of his office, walks along briskly, comes to a door, stops.

68 CLOSE SHOT OF DOOR

It is lettered SUPERINTENDENT J. McKECHNIE. Killaine knocks, then starts in without waiting for an answer.

69 INTERIOR OF McKECHNIE'S OFFICE

McKechnie is at his desk. He is a military-looking Scotch-Canadian, with a white mustache. Beside the desk sits an elderly, prim-looking man in a dark suit with a black tie. Killaine comes up to desk.

McKECHNIE
Killaine, this is Mr. Mitchell, Senior. Young Mitchell's father. He just flew in from Toronto.

KILLAINE
*(to Mitchell)*
How do you do, sir.

Mitchell nods.

> McKECHNIE

I've explained the situation to Mr. Mitchell up to a point. Now about this Mayfield girl?

> KILLAINE

She's a suspect, naturally. But not the only one.

> McKECHNIE
> *(harshly)*

She's the only one who had a dead man in her room. The only one who won't give an account of herself. The only one who tried to run away. And the only one, so far as I've been told, who went to such lengths to disguise her identity that she even removed the labels from her clothes. What more do you want?

> MITCHELL, SR.

She should have been arrested last night.

> McKECHNIE

That's as may be.
> *(to Killaine)*

We've ample grounds to detain her for questioning. You can't deny that, surely.

> KILLAINE

No.

> McKECHNIE

I hear she's a very pretty girl.

> KILLAINE

Which forces me to arrest her against my better judgment.

> McKECHNIE

Aye. You have a point there.

> MITCHELL, SR.

If so, I must say that it escapes my attention, Superintendent. It is my son who has been murdered. He was not in all ways a good son—but he was my son. I want his murderer punished. The girl's obviously a criminal of some sort. Otherwise, she'd give an account of herself. Arrest her, and you'll find out soon enough.

McKECHNIE
(eyeing Killaine)
I think he's right.

KILLAINE
(standing up)
Am I to interpret that as an order to arrest Miss Mayfield?

McKECHNIE
When I give you an order, you'll not need it interpreted.
(glances up at clock on wall)
You have an hour to make your mind up.
(he turns to Mitchell, Sr.)
Well, are ye satisfied, Mr. Mitchell?

MITCHELL, SR.
I'll be satisfied when my son's murderer is convicted and hanged.
(pause—his expression softens a little)
You've given this young man a very difficult choice.

McKECHNIE
Aye. That was the point you said you didn't get.
(he turns back to Killaine)
That's all.
(he makes a gesture of dismissal)

KILLAINE
Very good, sir.

He turns. We PAN HIM TO THE DOOR, he starts out.

70    INTERIOR CORRIDOR AS KILLAINE COMES FROM McKECHNIE'S OFFICE

Starts back towards his own office.

Another plain clothes cop, Driscoll, is walking towards Killaine. They meet just outside Killaine's office. Driscoll is a tall, solemn-looking Irishman.

> DRISCOLL
> May I have a moment, Inspector?

Killaine stops.

> DRISCOLL
> The Harbor police have just picked a dead man out of the water.

> KILLAINE
> Floater?

> DRISCOLL
> *Not* a floater. Only just dead.

> KILLAINE
> *(starting to turn away)*
> You're the waterfront specialist. Find out about it. I've got a murder to investigate.

> DRISCOLL
> You have two murders to investigate. This man's head was beaten in. And there's nothing in his pockets.

Killaine turns back, glances at his wrist watch.

> KILLAINE
> Drunk-rolling job. They hit him too hard.

> DRISCOLL
> *(annoyed with his manner)*
> I've been on the waterfront detail for twelve years. This man hadn't been dead an hour. He wasn't killed last night. He was killed today. In broad daylight. That's no drunk-rolling job.

KILLAINE
*(starting to turn away again)*
Let me know when you've identified him.

Driscoll gives him a somber look and starts to leave.

KILLAINE
*(calling after him)*
And don't get too logical, Driscoll. In police business it doesn't work. I wish it did. But it doesn't.

DRISCOLL
*(looking back)*
I'm an Irishman, sir. An Irishman is *always* logical.

Killaine frowns, then starts into his own little office.

71    CLOSE SHOT—A PORTION OF A TALL, SPEAR-TOPPED IRON RAILING ALONG A SIDEWALK

A man in a business suit is leaning against it. He is a plainclothes dick by the name of Handley. Other people are standing near him, looking through the railing, as if waiting for something to happen. Handley is looking in the other direction, along the sidewalk. In the background, SOME TRAFFIC NOISE, and far off, BLAST OF A TUG WHISTLE. Handley gets a cigarette out and lights it, with his eyes still looking off to the side. CAMERA PANS SLOWLY ALONG THE RAILING, showing people standing in groups looking through. CAMERA PICKS UP BETTY AMONG THEM. Near at hand, there is a SHARP WHISTLE BLAST, and immediately snare drums are HEARD, first in spaced tap, then going into a tattoo.

72    LONG SHOT—GRAVELLED OR PAVED SPACE IN FRONT OF AN OFFICIAL-LOOKING BUILDING,

built of stone, with broad steps. The Union Jack flies from a flagpole. On the space in front of the building, two small groups of soldiers are drawn up, and two bands. One group of soldiers is in battle dress, and the band which matches it is a bugle and drum band, also in battle dress. The other group is in the dress uniform of the Seaforth Highlanders, with kilts, Glengarrys, etc., and their band is a pipers' band, in kilts. What is taking place is a guard mount. (Subject to correct, as follows.) The old guard is stood at attention and inspected by the outgoing officer of the day, and during this inspection the drums and bugle band will march up and down in front of them, playing. The inspection over, the old guard will be formed into a marching column, the drum and bugle band will take position ahead of them, and the whole outfit will march across the parade ground and back again while the new guard stands at attention, its band silent. The old guard will then be halted, and faced towards the new guard, and will present arms. Then it will march off behind its band, while the kiltie guard is called to attention and presents arms. The outgoing and incoming officers of the day will salute each other. As the old guard marches off, their band will stop playing, and the pipers will march and start playing the bagpipes. This will continue while the new guard is inspected. Then the new guard will be marched off behind the pipes, and the ceremony is over. This is the background of the following scenes, and is going on all the time. Whatever portion of it is to be shown is immaterial, but the sound of it will be heard always, louder, not so loud, not loud at all, according to what is going on and how far off the bands are. Betty is staring through the railing as the drum and bugle band goes into its tattoo and starts marching. A moment later, the bugles join in.

CUT BACK TO

73   CLOSE-UP OF HANDLEY

He is looking off in the other direction, makes a signal.

74   WHAT HE SEES

A motorcycle officer standing beside the curb, near his motorcycle which has a side car.

75   CLOSE SHOT—RADIO DISPATCHER IN COMMUNICA-TIONS DIVISION OF POLICE HEADQUARTERS.

DISPATCHER
(into mike)
Go ahead, three-eight-six.

100

VOICE FROM LOUDSPEAKER
Party I am detailed to observe is watching guard mount in front of Parliament buildings. Sergeant Handley is standing by.

(NOTE: There are no Parliament Buildings in Vancouver. They are in Victoria, so some substitute must be found.)

DISPATCHER
*(into mike)*
Message received. Stand by. One-two-five.

He scribbles something on a pad, tears sheet off, and holds it out behind him without looking. A uniformed police officer takes it.

76     CLOSE SHOT OF BETTY—WATCHING THROUGH RAILING

77     WHAT SHE SEES—A PORTION OF GUARD MOUNT CERE-MONIAL

78     CLOSE SHOT OF HANDLEY

standing by railing, watching Betty. DRUM AND BUGLE MUSIC OVER SCENE.

79     EXTERIOR OF STREET—LONG SHOT

A crowd against railing, motorcycle officer in foreground. A car ENTERS SHOT, stops behind motorcycle.

80     CLOSE SHOT—CAR

Killaine gets out, crosses to motorcycle officer, who salutes him, then points out of scene.

KILLAINE
I'll take over now. Wait for Handley.

He starts walking CAMERA WITH HIM, comes up with Handley, leans against the railing beside him.

KILLAINE
I'm relieving you, Handley. Carry on with Gore at the hotel.

Handley gives Killaine a curious look.

101

HANDLEY

Very good, sir.

He goes out of shot. Killaine watches him, then moves along the railings (the guard mount ceremony is continuing all this time), comes up beside Betty.

KILLAINE

This isn't a very good place to talk.

BETTY

I don't want to talk.

KILLAINE

I've come here to arrest you for murder.

DRUM AND BUGLE MUSIC IN BACKGROUND STOPS.

VOICE OF COMMAND
(over scene—very sharp and military)
Guard HALT!

A SOUND OF STAMPING FEET, THEN SILENCE.

VOICE OF COMMAND
Right TURN!

A SOUND OF FEET, A STAMP, A SLAPPING OF HANDS AGAINST RIFLE SLINGS as guard brings its arms to order. Betty turns her head to look at Killaine.

BETTY

I expected nothing else.

KILLAINE

I might be able to save you, if I knew enough.

BETTY

You wouldn't even try.
(Killaine reacts, hurt)
There must be some copper in you, or you wouldn't be an inspector.

KILLAINE

There must be— but when I'm with you, I can't
find it.


VOICE OF COMMAND
(over scene)
Guard, Present ARMS!

APPROPRIATE SOUNDS ARE HEARD, THEN A ROLL
STARTS ON THE TRAP DRUMS.


KILLAINE
(turning and looking through railing)
Everybody loves a guard mount—except the
guard.
(he looks at his watch)
My boss gave me an hour to make up my mind.
The time's almost up.

For the first time in the scene, Betty turns and faces him.

I'm about to be very silly. A man passes a girl on
the street—a very lovely girl—his eyes meet her
eyes, and something reaches out and takes hold of
his heart—and then she goes on and is lost in the
crowd—and he says to himself, "There goes my
lost love"—and it's true—if he never sees her
again, it's still true. Of course, after a while, he
forgets—or almost forgets—because after a while
we forget almost everything.
(Betty is silent, staring at him)
But this man is a copper. He gets orders—routine
orders—to go to a place and investigate a murder—and everything points to a certain girl.


BETTY
Points very straight to her.


KILLAINE
He looks at the girl, looks into her eyes—


BETTY
What does he see?

103

KILLAINE

Palm trees against a sunset—waves breaking on a
coral reef—the Taj Mahal by moonlight—roses in
an English garden, just after a shower—
*(he grins wryly)*
Clichés, one and all—but good ones, with a lot of
mileage left in them—there's one thing he does *not*
see—murder—and murder was what he was sent
to find. Pretty ridiculous, isn't it?

BETTY

Very ridiculous.

KILLAINE

That's my hard luck—I'm man enough to tell you
about it—and not be sorry.

BETTY

What do your friends call you?—the ones that
know you very well?—and like you very much?

KILLAINE

They call me Jeff.

BETTY

Jeff. Shall we go now, Jeff, and get it over with?

KILLAINE

Not quite yet.
*(pause)*
We know who the gun belonged to. Margo West.
She told us this morning.
*(pause)*
It doesn't mean much. Mitchell took it away from
her. He had a habit of going through her bag.

BETTY

Looking for peanuts, I suppose.

KILLAINE

So Mitchell had handled it. Afterwards, Brandon
picked it up.

*(he glances at her)*
There's no indication you handled it.

BETTY

I always wear gloves when I shoot people. A bad joke—but better than tears.

KILLAINE
*(glancing at his watch again)*
Time's up. I'm off the case.
*(he takes a deep breath)*

BETTY

They'll only send someone else—who won't be so kind.

KILLAINE

That's something I can't spare you. But I won't do it myself.

BETTY

Because you think you're in love with me?

KILLAINE

I'm enough of a copper to do my duty. My boss made it tough for me. If I don't arrest you, I've gone soft. If I do, it's to save my face. I don't play those rules.

He breaks off. PIPE MUSIC SOUNDS OVER SCENE. Killaine raises his voice.

KILLAINE

You've got a couple of hours, maybe.

BETTY

To do what?

KILLAINE

I can't answer that.

BETTY

What will they do to *you*?

105

KILLAINE

That's their business. Can I drop you somewhere?

BETTY

You're still a police officer, Jeff.
*(pause)*
I saw you send those two men away. I know they were watching me.

Killaine stares at her silently.

BETTY

What are you going to do—toss your job into Puget Sound? Because I make you think of magnolias? I thought a policeman was something like a soldier. That his duty came first. However much he might happen to hate it.

KILLAINE
*(steadily)*
I've been a soldier, too. There's a difference. A policeman, like a judge, has a right to disqualify himself on proper grounds.

BETTY

What proper grounds?
*(pause)*
*(Killaine doesn't answer)*
You can't be in love with me. You hardly know me. I'm not in love with you.

KILLAINE

I know that.

BETTY

But even if you *were* in love with me.

KILLAINE
*(almost rudely)*
There's an empty taxi across the street. If you're so anxious, take it. He'll know the way to police headquarters.

                         BETTY
You do things the hard way, don't you?

                        KILLAINE
Sometimes.

                         BETTY
Not sometimes. Always. Just because it *is* the hard
way. You're that kind of man, Jeff.

                        KILLAINE
Goodbye, Betty.

Betty doesn't answer. She shakes her head slightly, stands
with a little smile on her face. He turns, goes quickly out of
scene. The guard mount ceremony ends. The crowd begins to
break up. Betty glances across the street, then starts out.

80a    CLOSE SHOT—AN EMPTY TAXICAB, THE FLAG UP

The driver is parked by the curb. He has been watching the
guard mount and now he is waiting for a fare. He sees one,
gets quickly out of the cab, opens his door as Betty COMES
INTO THE SHOT. She gets into the cab.

                       CAB DRIVER
Where to, Miss?

                         BETTY
Downtown somewhere—anywhere.

                       CAB DRIVER
Right you are, Miss.

Shuts a door, starts around his car, as we

DISSOLVE TO

81     INTERIOR OF McKECHNIE'S OFFICE

McKechnie behind his desk. Killaine standing across from
him. (We enter the middle of a scene.)

                        McKECHNIE
Are you a policeman or a soft-handed nincom-
poop?

                           107

KILLAINE

A little of both, sir, and perhaps not quite enough of either.

McKECHNIE

It won't look pretty on your record, Killaine. Where's the girl now?

KILLAINE

I don't know, sir.

McKECHNIE

Well, find out. Who's covering her?

KILLAINE

Nobody's covering her. I detached the officer assigned to that duty.

McKechnie comes slowly to his feet. His voice is very quiet, and very dangerous.

McKECHNIE

This girl is a murderess, Killaine.

KILLAINE

I disagree, sir. As Inspector in charge of the case I have the right to form that opinion, the right to act on it.

McKECHNIE

Ye have, have ye?

KILLAINE

We lifted seven fairly good prints from Miss Mayfield's toilet articles. Washington ought to teletype us within a few hours.

McKECHNIE
(In the same deadly quiet voice)
And in the meantime this girl goes where she pleases, does what she pleases?

KILLAINE
Yes, sir.

McKechnie's eyes go down to his desk. His hand goes slowly to a yellow telegraph form, face down. He turns it over, then lifts it and reads in a quiet, measured voice:

McKECHNIE
SUPERINTENDENT J. McKECHNIE, VANCOU-
VER POLICE DEPARTMENT. VANCOUVER, B.C.
REPLYING FOR YOUR F.P. TELETYPE CLASSIFI-
CATION NO 2684 INCOMPLETE. WE ADVISE
IDENTIFICATION POSSIBLE. ELIZABETH KIN-
SOLVING, ARRESTED GREENWATER, NORTH
CAROLINA, JANUARY 8, 1948, ON A CHARGE
OF MURDER. SIGNED, F.B.I., WASHINGTON,
D.C. H. CLEARY, INSPECTOR IN CHARGE.
*(McKechnie looks up and meets Killaine's eyes)*
Have ye any comment, Killaine?

KILLAINE
Identification on possible, sir. Not conclusive.

McKECHNIE
*(reaching down and picking up another telegram)*
SUPERINTENDENT J. McKECHNIE, VANCOU-
VER POLICE DEPARTMENT. REPLYING YOUR
INQUIRY ELIZABETH KINSOLVING. SUBJECT
WAS INDICTED, FIRST DEGREE MURDER HER
HUSBAND, LEE KINSOLVING, JANUARY THIS
YEAR. GUILTY VERDICT SET ASIDE BY PRESID-
ING JUDGE. PRISONER DISCHARGED. WHERE-
ABOUTS NOW UNKNOWN. FINGERPRINT
CLASSIFICATION—
*(he holds up the other telegram and looks at Killaine)*
An exact correspondence, Killaine.

Killaine stands white and silent.

McKECHNIE
*(dropping the F.B.I. telegraph and
continuing to read the other)*
PHYSICAL DESCRIPTION: AGE 26, HEIGHT 5

109

FEET 1⅜ INCHES: WEIGHT, 118 POUNDS: LIGHT BROWN HAIR: DEEP BLUE EYES: SMALL, PERFECTLY FORMED FEATURES: EARS AND EARLOBES SMALL: SLENDER BUILD: WEARS SIZE 4 AA SHOE: QUIET REFINED MANNER: NEW YORK ACCENT. NO CHARGES PENDING. NO PRIOR CRIMINAL RECORD. MAYFIELD, MOTHER'S MAIDEN NAME. AIR-MAILING YOU PHOTOGRAPHS TODAY. SIGNED HUBERT TOLLISON, CHIEF OF POLICE, GREENWATER, NORTH CAROLINA.
*(slowly McKechnie drops this wire on top of the other)*
She's bleached her hair, of course.
*(pause)*
Would your sensibilities be offended, if I sent out a general alarm to pick up this girl?

KILLAINE
I think you'd be entirely justified, sir.

McKECHNIE
*(with a sudden roar)*
But you still think she's innocent.

KILLAINE
I do.
*(he reaches into his pocket, takes out his badge, places it on the desk, on top of the two telegrams)*
I think you'd like to have this.

McKechnie looks down at it without expression, speaks very slowly.

McKECHNIE
I believe you won decorations during the war.

KILLAINE
Two.

McKechnie picks the badge up and holds it on the flat of his hand, looking down at it.

110

McKECHNIE

There are people in this world who don't think a police badge is a badge of honor. I'm not one of them.

KILLAINE

Nor I. That is why I gave it to you.

McKECHNIE

*(same tone)*

You're a young man. You're romantic. You think a pretty face and a clean conscience go together. You think a soft voice means a soft heart. You'll grow out of that.

KILLAINE

Not too far, I hope.

McKECHNIE

*(suddenly very Scotch, the harsh and eloquent Covenanter)*

This badge is not an old newspaper you cast down on the desk. It is not a thing you give up as of no value. It may be taken from you—and you may die defending it. But you'll not use it to make cheap dramatic gestures with.

*(pause; Killaine is rocked back on his heels)*

It's the naked steel of the sword of Justice: Put it back in your pocket and hold tight to it—and someday you might grow into a worthiness ye lack now.

Killaine reaches out and takes the badge. He looks down at it, his face bitter and ashamed.

McKECHNIE

Get out of here!

KILLAINE

What are my orders, sir?

McKECHNIE

You think I'm wrong about this bit of a girl. Go out and prove it against me!

Killaine steps back, salutes, wheels about and exits scene. McKechnie looks after him, expressionlessly. The door closes off. He presses a button. A uniformed officer enters. McKechnie holds the two telegrams towards him.

                    McKECHNIE
          Condense these for an immediate all-stations pick-
          up order.

82      INTERIOR. KILLAINE'S OFFICE

As he enters, crosses to his desk, takes a small, steel mirror out of a drawer and examines his chin. CAMERA MOVES TO AN OVER-SHOULDER SHOT. He moves the mirror back until his face is seen in it. There is a bitter smile on his mouth.

                    KILLAINE
          Kid Galahad. The Knight of the White Plume.
          Jesse Holmes, the fool killer. Boy, you look won-
          derful in a tank—with the turret closed.

During the speech, a door is opened off. Killaine looks up. Driscoll is standing inside the room.

                    DRISCOLL
          Got a moment, Inspector?

                    KILLAINE
               (we are now PULLED BACK
               INTO A WIDER SHOT)
          I've got a year. Or a second. I'm not sure which.

                    DRISCOLL
          You told me when we'd identified this fellow—

Killaine nods.

                    DRISCOLL
          We've done that. He's a San Francisco private eye.
          Name Martin J. Goble, G-O-B-L-E. Had initials in
          his hat and for once he lived where he bought it.
          Goble and Greer is the firm name.

KILLAINE
*(still a bit nasty)*
Swimming with his hat on? That's original.


DRISCOLL
If you'd seen the blood on his head—and somebody had to carry him out to sea—


KILLAINE
I understand. Pity to mess up a nice clean boat.


DRISCOLL
*(registering controlled anger at Killaine's manner)*
I got through to Greer, his partner in the detective
business. Greer won't give out.


KILLAINE
*(leaning back in his chair,*
*half closing his eyes)*
I'd suggest a telegram. Something like this: Chief
of Police, San Francisco. A licensed private detective named Martin J. Goble, address so-and-so,
has been found murdered within our jurisdiction.
His partner, name something-something Greer,
refuses to give us any information. Correction.
Refuses information necessary to our investiga-
tion. Can you assist? Signed Detective Sergeant
Driscoll, Vancouver, British Columbia, Police.
*(Killaine opens his eyes, looks at Driscoll)*


DRISCOLL
Send that?


KILLAINE
*(indifferently)*
Would you?


DRISCOLL
*(after a pause)*
If you're asking my opinion, no. I'd read it to Greer
over the phone. Ask *him* if he had any objections.

Killaine stands up, glances at his wristwatch.

113

KILLAINE

Catch me at the Vancouver Royal if it's important.

DRISCOLL

How important would it have to be? It's only murder, Inspector.

Killaine goes close to him, suddenly smiles.

KILLAINE

The Super's just given me the sweetest dressing down I've ever had. I'm still reeling from it. And believe me, I had it coming. I apologize. What *you* think is important—*I* think is important.

DRISCOLL
(*answering his smile*)

Thanks, Inspector. What are your orders about this wire to San Francisco?

KILLAINE

Men like you don't need orders.

He turns, exits scene. Driscoll is now smiling broadly.

DISSOLVE TO

83    INTERIOR OF BRANDON'S LIVING ROOM—EMPTY

The door opens, Brandon comes in, crosses in the direction of the bedroom.

84    INTERIOR. BRANDON'S BEDROOM.

Brandon comes in from living room, crosses to wall safe. His expression is tight, business-like, his movements quick, as if he had a lot to do and didn't intend to waste any time. Opens wall safe, takes a wad of currency from it, stuffs currency into breast pocket, relocks safe. A door buzzer SOUNDS to the door of his apartment. Brandon reacts, starts to exit.

85    INTERIOR. BRANDON'S LIVING ROOM

Brandon enters from bedroom. Door buzzer SOUNDS again. He picks up his hat and coat, goes to door, opens it. Killaine comes past Brandon into room, closing the door.

KILLAINE

Time for a little chat?


BRANDON

If it doesn't take too long. Drink?


KILLAINE

Thanks. I don't mind.

Brandon throws hat and coat on couch, crosses to liquor cabinet, begins to mix a couple of drinks; his back is now turned to Killaine, who saunters across room to French doors, exits to terrace. Brandon turns with the glasses in his hands, reacts, then starts after Killaine.

86    EXTERIOR. PENTHOUSE TERRACE

Killaine is standing against the wall in the corner, looking down at the point where the terrace overlooks Betty's balcony. Brandon enters from living room carrying glasses, reacts again, controls himself, crosses to Killaine.


BRANDON

Here you are.

Killaine turns, takes glass.


KILLAINE

Thanks. Lovely view you have, haven't you?


BRANDON

I never notice a view after the first week.


KILLAINE

I would. Fancy waking up every morning with that in your lap.
        (he gestures towards the view)
Wonderful thing, money is. Remember what Somerset Maugham said about it?


BRANDON

I wouldn't know.

KILLAINE

"Money is a sort of sixth sense that gives meaning to all the others." Very appealing, especially to a poor man.

BRANDON

Could we discuss that some other time?

KILLAINE

Sure. Let's discuss Betty Mayfield.
(pause)
How long since you saw her?

BRANDON

A couple of hours.

KILLAINE

I have a warrant for her arrest.

BRANDON

That must hurt.

KILLAINE

I've always thought you were a pretty nice guy, Brandon. I'd like to go on thinking so. If you tried to help her get away—

BRANDON

Would that make me a heel?

KILLAINE

You'd be breaking the law.

BRANDON

Doesn't answer the question.

KILLAINE

The only answer I have for you.

BRANDON

You passed up a dozen chances to arrest her. What toughened you up?

KILLAINE

Information.

BRANDON

Don't kid me. *You* don't think she murdered Mitchell.

KILLAINE

It could have been an accident.

BRANDON

That could be told.

KILLAINE

Not if she knew she wouldn't be believed.

BRANDON

You're concentrating too hard, Killaine. What about Margo West? She had a motive. I guess you know by this time whose gun it was?

Killaine nods.

BRANDON

And old man Clarendon? He had a motive, too— Margo and her money.

KILLAINE

Mitchell was killed down there.
(*he points*)
How could Clarendon get in to do it?
(*pause*)
Or Margo for that matter.

BRANDON

How could Mitchell? After that act he put on up here, is it likely she'd let him in?

KILLAINE

She didn't have to. He could have climbed down from here.

Brandon looks down over the wall. He turns, deadpan.

117

                    BRANDON
Mitchell was too drunk.

                    KILLAINE
Or just drunk enough. He was with her when she
registered. He knew where her room was. You
were out most of the evening. There was a lot of
mess to clean up. Waiters coming and going, the
door standing open. Suppose Mitchell came in to
grab a drink for himself, then wandered out on
this balcony, then realized Betty's balcony was just
belows yours.

                    BRANDON
Romeo in reverse. Uh-uh. No sale, Killaine.

                    KILLAINE
You don't buy it. Okay. So I still want Betty
Mayfield. Where is she?

                    BRANDON
No idea.

Phone rings off, in the living room.

                    BRANDON
Excuse me. My phone.

He turns, exits scene. Killaine stands a moment, looking
down from the edge of the terrace, then follows Brandon.

87   INTERIOR. PENTHOUSE LIVING ROOM—INCLUDING
PHONE AND TERRACE DOORS.

Brandon is just lifting receiver.

                    BRANDON
Hello.

His expression tightens, he glances quickly towards the
French doors as Killaine appears in them and strolls into the
living room. Brandon turns his back to Killaine.

                    118

BRANDON
*(into phone)*
Sorry. It's not very convenient just now.

88    INTERIOR—WAITING ROOM IN THE HUDSON BAY
COMPANY'S DEPARTMENT STORE.

Shoppers, men and women and children, etc., sitting
around. In the background a line of phone booths. CAMERA
PICKS OUT a deadpan, nondescript-looking man who might
be a dick as he stands up from a chair, crosses towards phone
booths, CAMERA WITH HIM. Phone booths are all full. He
stops before a booth, through the glass door of which Betty
can be seen on the phone. She catches his eye, turns away
quickly. The man nonchalantly lights a cigarette, leans against
the booth.

89    CLOSE SHOT

BETTY
*(into phone in booth)*
I had no right to call you anyway. I've made you
enough trouble. I—I think I know what to do—if
they'll let me.

Her eyes turn to look at the man waiting outside the booth.
He is not looking at her.

QUICK CUT TO

90    BRANDON ON PHONE

Killaine, behind him in a chair, has picked up a magazine.

BRANDON
*(casual voice)*
It sounds like a fair location. Could you be a little
more exact?

QUICK CUT TO

91    BETTY ON PHONE

BETTY
I'm in the Hudson Bay Company's store. That man
last night—the one that followed me—

119

CUT TO

92    BRANDON ON PHONE

BRANDON
I don't think that's on the market anymore. I'd like
something much closer to the water.

Killaine is listening, but he does not look up.

BRANDON
Can't be too close for me. Right across the street
from it suits me. Anything else listed?

93    INTERIOR—PHONE BOOTH

BETTY
*(into phone, low penetrating voice, her mouth
very close to mouthpiece)*
There's another man—right outside the booth
here. I never saw him before.

94    INTERIOR—BRANDON'S LIVING ROOM—BRANDON
ON PHONE

BRANDON
You're probably mistaken about that. Let's get
together and talk it over. There's always a solution
to these problems. But it must be near the water.
*Quite* near—
*(pause)*
Yes. If you don't mind waiting.

CUT TO

95    BETTY ON PHONE

Showing the man still standing outside the booth. He glances
in casually. Betty turns her head into phone.

BETTY
Close to the water. Like last night. I'll try. Goodbye.

She hangs up, stands a moment as if mustering her courage,
then turns.

120

96  INTERIOR—WAITING ROOM NEAR BETTY'S PHONE
    BOOTH

The man is standing there, smoking. Betty opens the door, comes out past him, not looking at him, then turns with quick decision and faces him.

> BETTY
> *(to man)*
> I'm sorry I kept you waiting.

> MAN
> *(he has his hand on the knob of the booth door,*
> *holding it. He smiles quickly)*
> Don't give it a thought, Miss. Matter of fact, waiting is my trade.

A big woman pushes past them, starts to heave herself into the booth he is about to enter. The man reacts smoothly.

> MAN
> *(to big woman)*
> Pardon me, Madam. Is that your handkerchief?

He points to a spot on the floor behind her. She steps back and turns. He glides into the booth, draws the door shut, winks at Betty through the glass. Betty hides her face as she turns away. The big woman is furious.

97  INTERIOR—BRANDON'S LIVING ROOM

He has just left the phone and crossed to make another drink. Killaine tosses the magazine aside and stands up.

> KILLAINE
> No more for me, thanks. Remember what I said. You can't interfere with the law.

> BRANDON
> Where would she go, anyway? Don't tell me you haven't got her covered.

Killaine just looks at him, then nods, turns away.

BRANDON

Mitchell was a heel. We both know that. Why take it for granted that somebody in the hotel knocked him off?

Killaine doesn't answer.

BRANDON

You forgot the gag line, Killaine. The police don't take anything for granted.

KILLAINE

I'm afraid they do. Far too often. So long.

BRANDON

Wait a minute. I'll go with you.

Crosses, picks up hat and coat, reaches Killaine at the door. They start out.

DISSOLVE TO

98    INTERIOR—ELEVATOR DESCENDING IN MOTION

BRANDON AND KILLAINE

KILLAINE
(casually)
You do a lot of real estate trading, Brandon?

BRANDON

Now and then. Mostly just for the fun of it.

KILLAINE

I tried it once. I lost my shirt.

BRANDON
(with a faint smile)
I buy my shirts by the dozen. Fortunately.

KILLAINE
(glancing at the operator)
Where did it all come from? Or is that a permissible question?

122

Elevator stops. Other people get in. Elevator starts down again.

WIPE TO

99     INTERIOR—LOBBY BY ELEVATOR

Elevator reaches lobby floor, doors open, people come out, Killaine and Brandon separately. Brandon first. He waits for Killaine.

> BRANDON
> I had a father who knew how to steal.

> KILLAINE
> *(puzzled)*
> What?

> BRANDON
> You asked me where it all came from.

> KILLAINE
> *(smiles)*
> Oh. That was just one of those idle questions. One doesn't expect an answer.

Brandon nods, turns towards the desk, Killaine following. Campbell, the manager, is behind the desk, and a clerk. The clerk, seeing Brandon, reaches mail out of box, hands it to Brandon, who stands looking it over.

> KILLAINE
> *(to Campbell)*
> I think I'd like to take another look at Mr. Mitchell's room.

Brandon glances at him quickly, then back to his mail.

> KILLAINE
> I don't know why. As a matter of fact, I don't know anything.

> CAMPBELL
> *(polite but rather cold)*
> It's about time you *did*—know something.

KILLAINE

I agree with you perfectly. But when did time ever
help a fool?

Brandon gives another quick glance, then strolls off along the
lobby towards the main hotel entrance, still looking at his
mail as he walks. Killaine looks after him.

100     ANOTHER ANGLE

Killaine goes over to where Handley is sitting, drops into a
chair beside him, takes out his crested cigarette case, takes a
cigarette, then with an after-thought, offers the case to
Handley, which brings them close together, as Handley takes
cigarette.

HANDLEY

Nothing. She hasn't shown.

KILLAINE

Check the boat?

HANDLEY

Gore's out doing it now.

Killaine gives him a light. They both puff. Killaine puts
cigarette case away.

KILLAINE
(pretending to stifle a yawn)
Must be almost tea-time.
(moves to get up)
I'll be in Mitchell's room.

Handley nods slightly. Killaine gets up, starts to move back to
the desk. Campbell stands there waiting for him.

DISSOLVE TO

101     EXTERIOR. STREET NEAR WATERFRONT—BETTY WALK-
ING SLOWLY, CAMERA FOLLOWING

Her hands are deep in the pockets of her coat, head bent
forward. She comes under a street sign, looks up. The sign
says FRONT STREET. SOUND of a car coming up behind her.

SOUND indicates it is braking to a stop. Betty becomes rigid, then very slowly turns her head, as though she expected to find a police car had come up behind her.

BRANDON'S VOICE (OFF SCREEN)

Hop in.

102   ANOTHER ANGLE

Showing Brandon's convertible, Brandon leaning out. Betty crosses the sidewalk, gets into the car. HOLD ON THE CAR as it starts up, SHOOTING FROM A NATURAL ANGLE.

BETTY

I hated to go to that place. I almost went to the police station instead.

BRANDON

No percentage in that.

BETTY

They're going to arrest me.

BRANDON

I know. Killaine has a warrant.

BETTY

*(as the car turns into Front Street)*
I have my own warrant. Stop a minute, please.

Brandon looks at her, puzzled, brings the car to a stop; sits staring at her. Background of harbor, ships, Betty draws something out of her pocket—a paper—and hands it to him. He takes it, opens it, reads it aloud, in a low voice.

BRANDON

Dear Inspector Killaine: This is goodbye. You were right, I had a secret. You were right, I changed my name. I tried to hide from the past and I walked into almost the same situation that I had run away from. I didn't kill Larry Mitchell, but I can't prove it. I couldn't prove it the other time, either. Where I am going, nothing has to be proved. There's a lot of water between Vancouver and the U.S.A. In

125

that, and in you, Vancouver has been kind to me. I think you will understand. Betty Mayfield.

Brandon stops reading, his face is tight and grim. Slowly he refolds the note and turns to look at Betty.

> BRANDON
> If you meant it, you wouldn't show it to me, Betty.
> *(pause)*
> Or am I supposed to deliver it to dear Inspector Killaine?

> BETTY
> *(in a half-wild tone)*
> I wrote it in the waiting room of the Hudson Bay Store. With somebody's Pekingese trying to climb into my lap. Perhaps you're right. Perhaps I didn't mean it. All I know is that I'm licked.

> BRANDON
> *(very slowly)*
> There's a lot of water between Vancouver and the U.S.A. This note is a suicide note. After you're gone, where would they look for you?
> *(long pause)*
> *Why* would they look for you? Darkness, and open water, and a fast cabin cruiser. And I have a pocket full of money. And if I helped you, I'd be committing a crime, or so they tell me.

> BETTY
> That wasn't why I called you. Why did I hope— when I hadn't any right to hope?

> BRANDON
> How bad is it? Bad enough for—
> *(he taps the note)*

> BETTY
> Yes. I've never been very far from it, for a long time. Will you do something nice for me?

Brandon nods.

126

BETTY

Take me where I haven't the courage to take
myself.

BRANDON

How bad is the other thing? The secret?

BETTY

I was tried for murdering my husband. Guilty. The
judge set the verdict aside. There was one man on
the jury—
(she pauses, shakes her head)
—but he was afraid. They were all afraid—of my
father-in-law. That man that was following me last
night—he came from *him* of course. My father-in-
law will never give up. Never. He promised me
that.
(she laughs a little)
So I came to Vancouver, B.C. As far away as I can
get from North Carolina. And it happens all over
again. Almost the same thing. Almost the same
way. Do you wonder about this—

She reaches to take the note from his hand. He pulls it away
from her.

BRANDON

This is the ace, Betty. But not of spades. They'll
find out about the other. They might know already.
And when they get this—
(he holds the note up again)
What would they look for? Where? Out there
somewhere?
(he points towards the open
water beyond the ships)

BETTY

They'll look for *you*.

BRANDON

I run over to Victoria. Play some golf with people I
know. Do it all the time. That's why I have a cabin
cruiser. Custombuilt. Forty knots. Mr. Clark Bran-

127

don, an almost gentleman of almost complete leisure. Member of six golf clubs. Broke 70 once on the Shaughnessy Heights Course. You have to be good to do that. And if you look out of a front window of the Empress Hotel in Victoria, in a few hours you can look right down on Mr. Brandon's boat, the Valkyrie. Came alone? Sure. He always comes alone. Mr. Brandon's a rather lonely man.

                    BETTY
          (staring at him, fascinated)
And Betty Mayfield—

                  BRANDON
Blonde, beautiful, and sad—and nowhere. Of course she might have run away—if she knew how. And where to go. She might have dyed her hair. Bleached it before probably.
          (Betty nods)
And changed her name again. But look at this note.
          (he holds it up)
And look at her room in the hotel. Her stuff is all there. Hasn't a rag except what she stood up in. You don't run away like that. Not if you are young and beautiful. No chance.

                    BETTY
     (catching a little enthusiasm from him)
But that's what I *am* doing. Couldn't *they* think of that?

                  BRANDON
If they had any reason to. Why make it tough for themselves? Why go to all that trouble? Here's an open book. Close it. No reason to keep it open. She was a nice girl, anyway. And perhaps she didn't kill him on purpose. Perhaps she didn't kill that other one. You never know. Give her the benefit of the doubt. Leave her stay where she is. Close the book. Finis.

                    128

BETTY
Killaine . . .

BRANDON
The best interference runner we've got. He thinks
he's in love with you—and he's a gentleman. Come
here, Baby.

He pulls her towards him, holds her in his arms, and kisses
her.

BRANDON
*I'm* not. Or I wouldn't be doing this right now.
*(softly)*
Even if I didn't like you, I'd have to do it. Like the
guy that was dealt thirteen spades in a bridge
hand. Or filled an ace-high flush. You couldn't get
him out of that game to give him the Pulitzer Prize.

They pull apart. Brandon starts the car again. As it gets into
motion, he looks forward through the windshield, brakes
suddenly, with a grim expression.

103    WHAT HE SEES—SHOOTING FORWARD THROUGH THE
       WINDSHIELD OF THE CAR

Along the block, at the end of which is Charlie's Place. The
sign can be made out vaguely. A police car stands in front of
the door.

104    BACK TO BRANDON AND BETTY

BRANDON
*(with forced carelessness)*
Must be raid day at Magruder's. They always raid
him before he opens, so he won't lose any business.

105    WIDER SHOT—EXTERIOR OF THE CAR

As Brandon turns it in a fast U-turn, CAMERA PANS IT OUT
OF SIGHT IN THE OPPOSITE DIRECTION, THEN PANS
BACK TO PICK UP THE POLICE CAR IN FRONT OF
MAGRUDER'S. Go to a CLOSE SHOT of the police car.
Uniformed chauffeur at the wheel. One of the car doors is
standing open. PAN TO THE ENTRANCE OF CHARLIE'S.

129

Another uniformed cop is standing at the door. He pushes the door open, looks inside, up the staircase. CAMERA PANS TO SHOOT UP THE DARK, EMPTY STAIRS.

WIPE TO

106     INTERIOR. CHARLIE'S.

As seen before, except that the place is now tidied up, the tables are in order, arranged for the night. A door at the back opens and a plain clothes dick, one we have not yet seen, comes through, starts walking rapidly in the direction of the street stairs. Through the open door we hear Driscoll's voice.

> DRISCOLL'S VOICE (OFF SCREEN)
> (not too loud)
> I want a man from the I-Bureau down here as soon as possible. There's some stuff in the waste basket I'm afraid to handle.

CUT TO

107     INTERIOR. MAGRUDER'S OFFICE.

As Driscoll replaces phone, turns to face Magruder, who is handcuffed, with a man standing beside him. Magruder is scowling. Driscoll brings up his left hand, showing on a spread handkerchief the sawed-off belly gun that Magruder took away from Goble and put in his desk drawer.

> DRISCOLL
> What always throws me about people like you is that you're so stupid. Don't you know these things have numbers on them? And that they have to be registered if they're owned legally? And that if we find a man dead with his pockets empty—and identify him and find out he's a private detective from San Francisco—

> MAGRUDER
> (tough)
> It needs music.

130

DRISCOLL
*(ignoring him and continuing right on)*
—all we have to do is call the San Francisco Police
to get the numbers of his guns. For the love of the
Saints, Magruder, if you're going into the murder
business, why don't you learn a few rules? You
must have been pretty desperate to move him out
of here in broad daylight.

Magruder reacts. This one catches him right square on the
point of his chin.

DRISCOLL
*(softly)*
Don't you know we have people down in this
district working for us? They might look like
tramps to you, and some of them are. But they
have eyes.

MAGRUDER
*(hoarsely)*
The guy pulled a gun on me. I thought it was a
stick-up. I hit him with a sap. Why wouldn't I?
Maybe I hit him too hard, and it scared me. I
wanted to get him away from here. A guy like me
don't always get believed by guys like you.

DRISCOLL
You had over sixteen hundred dollars in your
pocket, a thousand of them in twenty-dollar bills.
With a kind of new look about them at that. Would
you be interested in what I think about this,
Magruder?

Magruder doesn't answer. He is beginning to look very
groggy.

DRISCOLL
*(sharply, to the other dick)*
Hold him. He's trying to sag on us.

The other dick straightens Magruder up, pushes him against
the wall. Magruder's eyes are rolling in his head.

131

DRISCOLL
*(mercilessly)*
This man Goble rented the car, gave a false name.
He had no license, no identification. But he put up
a sufficient deposit. He was a suspicious man. He
was on a dubious errand. He had a gun in his
pocket and I'm thinking one of these manila
envelopes—
*(he points to the waste basket)*
—contained those sheets of blank paper which he
was going to sell for money. And get out before
anybody looked at what he sold. You had the
money, Magruder. But you didn't give it to him.
You killed him instead.

Magruder starts to sag again.

DRISCOLL
*(more gently)*
Perhaps you didn't mean to kill him. But here he
was dead, and his car was outside in the street. So
you brought it around to the alley and you carried
the man down to it, and you drove him away. And
what happened to him after that, nobody knows
until he was picked out of the water of the Sound,
dead. But not long dead. Where did you leave the
car, Magruder? Who helped you? What boat did
you have?
*(pause. His voice changes to a dry, businesslike tone,
addressing the other dick)*
All right. Take him in. Set him down. Give him
what he wants to make him comfortable. And get a
stenographer. And warn him. And don't rough
him. He's a nice little man. All he wants is to collect
his thoughts. And then he'll tell us the whole story
in his own words.
*(his voice becomes positively corny)*
Won't you, Magruder, darling?

Magruder pitches forward to the floor in a dead faint. The
two detectives stand looking down at him.

DRISCOLL
*(somberly)*
He'll be giving the priest a bad time, will this one.
Maybe         you'd              better
call an ambulance. He might have a wonky ticker.

132

108    EXTERIOR OF VANCOUVER YACHT CLUB BUILDING—
       PARKING SPACE IN FRONT

       CAMERA PICKS OUT BRANDON'S SEDAN which has just
       parked. Brandon and Betty are getting out.

109    CLOSER SHOT—BRANDON AND BETTY

                          BRANDON
              Over this way.

       They start towards the corner of the building away from the
       entrance.

110    NARROW WOODEN WALK ALONG THE SIDE OF THE
       YACHT CLUB BUILDING

       Yacht Anchorage in the background. To one side a row of
       covered mooring slips, with a wooden walk behind them.
       BRANDON AND BETTY COME INTO THE SHOT, WALK-
       ING.

111    THE WALK BEHIND THE MOORING SLIPS

       Brandon stops at a padlocked door, unlocks it, opens it. They
       start through.

112    INTERIOR OF BOATHOUSE—SEMI-DARKNESS

       The seaward end is open, a big cabin cruiser is moored in the
       slip, a wooden ladder going down to it. Brandon goes down
       ladder to deck of cruiser, steadies it by pulling on the line,
       helps Betty down, then down into the cockpit.

113    INTERIOR OF COCKPIT, SHOOTING INTO CABIN DOWN
       A SHORT COMPANIONWAY

       Brandon loads Betty down the companionway to the cabin of
       the cruiser. It is paneled, with curtained windows, luxurious.

                          BRANDON
              You'll be safe here. I won't be long.
                   (puts a bunch of keys on the table)
              Help yourself to anything you want. The galley's
              through there.
                   (he points to a door up forward)
              You can make coffee if you like.

BETTY
*(looking around her)*
This must have cost a fortune.

BRANDON
It did, but it never paid off—until now.
*(he looks at his watch)*
I ought to be back within an hour. We can't leave
until near dark anyway.

BETTY
Do you *have* to leave the note?

BRANDON
It's the frame on the picture. But not if you say not.

He takes note out of his pocket and holds it out. Betty doesn't
touch it.

BRANDON
I'd still go through—even if I ended up in jail.

BETTY
You wouldn't like it. I've been there.

BRANDON
*(quietly)*
My father died in jail, and he was twice the man I
am.

Betty just stares at him.

BRANDON
*(holding up the letter)*
Well?

BETTY
*(in a choked voice)*
You leave it.

She turns away quickly. Brandon stands a moment, looking at
her, then turns back and EXITS SCENE.

WIPE TO

114 INTERIOR. POLICE CAR IN MOTION—SHOOTING FOR-WARD

Police radio is on. From it:

VOICE FROM RADIO
C.V.P.L. Vancouver Police Department. Repeating. All Points Bulletin No. 611. General alarm. Wanted for questioning. A young woman. American. Using the name Betty Mayfield, formerly Elizabeth Kinsolving of Greenwater, North Carolina. Height five feet one and a half inches. Weight 118 pounds. Hair blonde, may be dyed darker. Blue eyes. Slender build. Size 4AA shoes. Quiet refined manner. Any person answering this description should be held. Communicate immediately with Superintendent J. McKechnie, Vancouver City Police, Vancouver, B.C., for F.P. Classification.

CUT TO

115 INTERIOR OF MITCHELL'S ROOM, VANCOUVER ROY-AL—CLOSE SHOT

A handsome table radio, Gore standing beside it. The continuation of broadcast in previous scene, without break, but with a difference in tone, due to the different instrument.

VOICE FROM RADIO
Outlying cities and towns please rebroadcast. Coast Guard stations please rebroadcast. Suspect may attempt to cross border. C.V.P.L. Vancouver City Police, Vancouver, B.C. I will repeat this bulletin.

Gore reaches across, shuts radio off, turns, CAMERA PULLS BACK TO A WIDER SHOT OF MITCHELL'S ROOM which is a typical, not very expensive hotel room, but with some personal furniture such as table lamps, a shelf of books, a few indications that this has become the home of someone. Gore moves towards the bed, where Killaine is going through the contents of a suitcase. He has underwear, shirts, socks, etc., spread out all around the suitcase on the bed cover.

GORE

She didn't seem the type to lam out—even if she
got the chance. That stuff was all gone through last
night. Anything special you're looking for, Inspector?

KILLAINE

I'll know when I find it.

GORE

I guess I'm just ballast around here.

Killaine doesn't answer. He straightens up with a very fancy
thin gold cigarette case in his hand. He opens it.

GORE

You get those from rich women—if you are the
kind of guy Mitchell was.

Killaine dumps the cigarettes out of the case and holds the
inside against the light. His gaze becomes fixed.

KILLAINE
(reading)
G.G. Market one-eight-four-two.

GORE

Gigi, huh? Sounds French—one of those fancy
ladies. Must have been *very* fancy, if he scratched
her phone number in gold.

KILLAINE
(ignoring him, speaking to himself)
Market . . . It seems to me that's a San Francisco
exchange.

116     INTERIOR. BEER TAVERN IN A BASEMENT—ARTIFICIAL
LIGHT

(NOTE: I am assuming that only beer may be sold on the
premises in Vancouver.) Brandon is seated at a small table,
with a bottle and glass of beer in front of him. He takes Betty's
suicide note out of his pocket, rereads it. CAMERA MOVES
IN ENOUGH TO SHOW WHAT HE IS READING. He refolds

it, holds it a moment, lost in thought, then puts it away in his pocket, glances at his wrist watch, stands up, starts out of scene, leaving the beer almost untasted.

117 INTERIOR OF BETTY'S ROOM AT THE VANCOUVER ROYAL

As Killaine comes in. He moves noiselessly around the room, glancing at this and that, goes into closet, comes back with an over-night case, which he puts on the bed. It is locked. He gets out a bunch of keys, tries two or three, opens it. He searches inside the over-night bag and comes up with a packet of travellers' checks. MOVE IN ON THEM TO SHOW THE DENOMINATIONS OF $500 and that the packet is quite a thick wad. Killaine replaces them in the over-night bag, relocks it, puts it back in the closet, starts out towards balcony.

118 INTERIOR. CABIN CRUISER—VERY DIM

Betty is stretched out on a bunk, smoking. NOISE is heard off, creaking of wood steps. She jumps to her feet, starts toward the companionway.

119 COCKPIT OF CRUISER

As Brandon comes down off ladder and Betty comes up companionway.

> BRANDON
> (tightly)
> Killaine's wise. We can't wait any longer. Here, put this on.
> (he opens locker, picks out an oilskin coat, hands it to her)
> But stay out of sight until we clear the harbor. I'll tell you when.
> (gets another oilskin out of locker, puts it on himself)

> BETTY
> Killaine's wise to what?

Without answering, Brandon slips past her, down companionway.

120 INTERIOR. CABIN

As Brandon enters, peeling off his overcoat and jacket, tosses overcoat and hat aside, opens locker with pushback door,

137

hangs jacket up inside, takes out a heavy sweater which he slips on, then a seamen's pea jacket which he also puts on. He reaches far in and comes out holding a .38 automatic, slips it into the inside pocket of the pea jacket, pulls locker door closed, starts out.

121    COCKPIT OF CRUISER

Betty has put on the oilskin coat as Brandon comes up companionway, slips behind the wheel and starts the motors. He yells something at her, but the roar of the motors drowns it out. He points. She nods, goes back down companionway. Brandon casts off, cruiser starts to back out of the slip.

122    EXTERIOR. YACHT ANCHORAGE—DAY

Cruiser backs in towards CAMERA, swings around, starts in a wide curve towards the harbor entrance, moving very fast. Brandon alone is seen. The cruiser picks up still more speed and heads off into the distance.

WIPE TO

123    LOBBY OUTSIDE BRANDON'S PENTHOUSE

Elevator comes up, opens, Campbell and Gore come out. Campbell crosses to penthouse door, presses bell, then turns to Gore.

> CAMPBELL
> I'm getting a little tired of this, Sergeant. Mr. Brandon's a valued guest in this hotel. We've known him for a long time. I don't like this prowling into people's rooms.

He presses the bell again.

> GORE
> How many people in your hotel know a man was murdered here, Mr. Campbell? Apart from you and the people we questioned?

> CAMPBELL
> (shortly)
> None, so far as I know.

138

GORE

And you don't like our methods, huh?

Campbell gives him a look, takes out passkey, and unlocks door, starts in. Gore moves past him, turns and blocks him.

GORE

That's all. Thanks, Mr. Campbell.

CAMPBELL

I insist—

GORE

That's all. Thanks, Mr. Campbell.

He pushes the door shut, pushing Campbell out with it. He puts on the night latch, grins, starts across living room to French doors to terrace.

CUT TO

124    EXTERIOR. BETTY'S BALCONY

Killaine standing, looking up the end wall towards the wall of the penthouse terrace. He looks down at the chaise on which Mitchell's body was found. He goes to it, wheels it over so it is close to the end wall. His eyes measure the distance from the chaise up to the top of the parapet wall of the penthouse terrace. Gore appears IN THE SHOT ABOVE. He looks down.

KILLAINE
(calling up to him)

I'm coming up.

He goes to the corner of the balcony wall, steps up on it, steadying himself with a hand against the steep end wall. He turns his body so that he is standing sideways, rather unsteadily, and reaches up. His hands are about two feet short of being able to reach the top of the wall at which Gore stands. Killaine gathers himself for a jump, springs, catches the top of the wall with one hand, swings outwards, glances down.

125    WHAT HE SEES

Sheer drop of 100 feet to the stone terrace outside the hotel lobby.

139

126    UPWARD ANGLE SHOT SHOWING KILLAINE DAN-
       GLING BY ONE HAND

Gore reaching down for him. Killaine's body swings in again.
With a jerk he gets the other hand up, laboriously pulls
himself up, and walks up the wall, CAMERA FOLLOWING
HIM. Gore reaches to help him.

                    KILLAINE
            *(tightly, straining with effort)*
       I'm all right.

He gets a leg over the penthouse wall, breathing hard.

127    EXTERIOR. PENTHOUSE BALCONY—REVERSE SHOT
       FROM THE PRECEDING ONE

Gore is standing by the wall, Killaine astride of it. He gets
over on to the balcony floor, stands up, wipes his hands off.

                     GORE
                   *(shaken)*
       That's pretty risky business, Inspector.

                    KILLAINE
       Somebody did it twice last night—in the dark.

He points down. Gore looks over the wall, downwards.

128    WHAT HE SEES

Portion of Betty's balcony and the chaise almost directly
below him.

            KILLAINE'S VOICE (OFF SCREEN)
       Once to put that in the position where it is now.
       And the second time to move it where we found it.

129    TWO SHOT—KILLAINE AND GORE

On the balcony.

                    KILLAINE
       Not too hard, is it?

                     GORE
                 *(staring at him)*
       Maybe we've been pretty dumb—

140

KILLAINE
*(quietly)*
There wasn't any motive . . . let's try out the act.

Gore steps back. Killaine puts his hand in his pocket and brings out a gun, which looks very like the death gun.

KILLAINE
I have a gun. It's not loaded. Pretend it is. I'm drunk. I took this gun away from Margo West. Now I've said something to you that you don't like. I don't like the look in your eyes, either. I've pulled the gun. Take it away from me. And while you're taking it away from me, it goes off. Ready?

Gore nods.

KILLAINE
Let's go.

Gore suddenly swarms him. There is a brief, sharp struggle. Gore gets his hand over the gun. It goes down as they fight for it. Gore turns it in towards Killaine's body. There is a sharp click. Gore steps back with the gun in his hand.

KILLAINE
Was that about the right angle?

GORE
I think so.

KILLAINE
Where's the shell?

GORE
Should be over there.

Points to the angle of the wall.

KILLAINE
Pick it up. Put it in your pocket.

Gore pretends to do so.

141

KILLAINE

The same with the gun.

Gore puts the gun in his pocket.

KILLAINE

You've got a dead man on your hands. You killed
him—even if it wasn't murder. What are you going
to do about it?

GORE

If I've got any sense I'm going to call Headquarters.

KILLAINE

They'll probably believe you. But they'll want to
know what you were fighting about. Why Mitchell
had a gun. You'll tell them a simple story. They'll
pretend it sounds all right to them. Now *you're*
Headquarters. How does it sound to *you*?

GORE

Before I took the story and closed the case, I'd
want to know a lot more about these people. I'd
want to know just about everything about them.

KILLAINE
*(nodding)*

Exactly. Now *I'm* the killer. And there's something
I don't want you to know. Something that would
destroy my comfortable life, rob me of my friends,
my position.

GORE

Such as?

KILLAINE

Assume there *is* something to hide. I go to a lot of
trouble. What do I do? What would *you* do?

GORE

Do I know who lives down there?
*(indicating the balcony below)*

142

KILLAINE

You can find out.

GORE

Do I know that she's out of the room? Likely to be out of it for some time?

KILLAINE

You can find out the first part. The second part you have to take a chance on.

GORE

Pretty big chance, huh?

KILLAINE

You've got a dead man on your hands. Like this.

He allows himself to collapse down on the floor, inert, against the wall.

GORE

Right—

He bends down over Killaine, gets a fireman's lift on him— gets him up, drapes him over the wall, half on one side and half on the other, his head and shoulders on the inside. He staightens up, takes a firm grip on Killaine's wrists, and eases him down over the wall. Gore's head and shoulders follow until he is lying across the wall on his stomach.

130    UPWARD REVERSE SHOT FROM BETTY'S BALCONY

Showing Killaine's body dangling directly over the chaise. Gore comes as far down as he can. Killaine has only a few feet to fall. Killaine looks down, then up at Gore.

KILLAINE

Let go.

Gore releases his wrists. Killaine sprawls down on the chaise, almost rolls off it, saves himself, lies down on his side. Gore climbs over the wall, lowers himself, hangs by his hands, looks down, lets go with one hand, drops, lands rather heavily on the balcony near the chaise, goes down on his hands and knees. He stands up, dusts himself off, lifts the

143

chaise with Killaine on it, and wheels it about six feet away to the position where it was found with Mitchell's body. Killaine stands up off the chaise.

KILLAINE

Next?

Gore reaches into his pocket, takes out the gun and a match.

GORE
(holding the match up)
This is the shell.
(tossing it over in the corner)
What about the gun?

KILLAINE

Well, what about it?

GORE

I've handled it. Mitchell's handled it. If I wipe it off, no suicide. If I take it out and lose it, no suicide. If I leave it here . . . no suicide.

KILLAINE

So?

GORE

I've got to find a way to handle it, openly. Like Brandon.

Killaine nods.

GORE
(doubtful again)
How did he know he'd get the chance? He couldn't have arranged it.

KILLAINE

He could have tried. If he was up there in the dark, listening, he'd know when she came home, know when she found Mitchell dead, know what she did about it. If she telephoned, he'd probably hear that.

GORE

And she *did* give him the chance, the way it
worked out.

KILLAINE

If she didn't—if luck was against him—he wipes
the gun off, reaches over the wall up there—drops
it on the chaise.

GORE

No suicide.

KILLAINE

Did we ever really think it was suicide?

GORE

You win, Inspector. You win all along the line.
Why didn't we think of Brandon before—or did
we—some of us?
                    (pause, then answering himself)
Yeah. Of course you did. When a suspect thinks
he's safe, you go on letting him think he's safe.
Wait for a mistake.

KILLAINE

And a motive—which we haven't got. So this
could all be a dream.

Gore nods silently. Killaine reaches in his pocket, takes out
Mitchell's thin gold case, opens it, looks down.

KILLAINE

Market one-eight-four-two.

He looks up at Gore.

GORE

Greer and Goble in the Call Building, San Francisco. Just like you thought . . . Two murders in
two days. Different places, different methods,
different people. Nothing connects them, but a
telephone number.

145

KILLAINE
*(softly)*
A thin wire—but very, very strong. Let's get out of here.

As they start out,

WIPE TO

131    LONG SHOT—OPEN WATER

Cabin cruiser coming into the SHOT at high speed.

132    CLOSER SHOT—CABIN CRUISER

Brandon is behind the wheel, Betty beside him. She is looking back over her shoulder.

BRANDON
See anything?

BETTY
I can still see the shoreline. The moon is rising.

BRANDON
There *would* be a moon tonight.

Betty shivers a little.

BRANDON
Cold?

BETTY
Frozen.

BRANDON
Go down into the cabin and get yourself a drink. Careful how you go, we're hitting the swell now.

Betty starts to move from the seat towards the companionway.

133    INTERIOR OF CABIN

As Betty comes in. The cruiser has begun to pitch and roll. She makes her way along the cabin. The cruiser gives a lurch, Betty is thrown off balance. She grabs a door handle. Door is pulled open. Clothes are seen hanging inside. The cruiser gives another lurch and Betty is thrown the other way, almost into the closet. Her hand plunges in among the clothes. Her expression shows she has touched something that startles her.

134    SHOOTING INTO THE CLOSET

Betty separates clothes and we see an empty gun holster hanging on a hook against the back wall of the closet. She stands motionless, staring at it, then notices Brandon's jacket hanging untidily on a hook with the inside pocket exposed and a corner of her own suicide note showing. CAMERA MOVES IN TO SHOW ENOUGH OF THE OUTSIDE OF THE ENVELOPE AND BETTY'S HANDWRITING to establish the fact. Betty's hand comes forward INTO THE SHOT. She draws the envelope from the pocket.

135    INTERIOR. CABIN

As Betty closes the closet door, crosses to bunk. The cruiser is pitching. She stands holding the suicide note envelope, finally turns it over, draws out the note, replaces it. Then, with a quick movement, she starts towards companionway.

136    INTERIOR. COCKPIT OF CRUISER—SHOOTING BACK TOWARDS THE BOILING WAKE

Brandon is staring straight ahead of him, tight-lipped. There is a distant SOUND OF A PLANE. Brandon looks up, searching the sky without changing expression. Betty comes back up the companionway, sits down in a corner of the seat.

BETTY
I decided I didn't want a drink . . . I'm beginning to wonder.

BRANDON
Wonder what?

BETTY
If you're doing all this just for me.

BRANDON
That, and the fun of it.

147

BETTY

I thought you had to go back to the hotel. To leave
my—my note.

BRANDON

That's right.

Silently Betty takes out the note and holds it towards him.
Brandon glances at it. He cocks his ear towards the PLANE
NOISE.

BRANDON

See anything up there?

As Betty looks up, he lets go of the wheel, and makes a
sudden grab for the wrist of the hand holding the note. There
is a short, sharp struggle. Brandon has the note. The wheel
swings wildly and the cabin cruiser keels over into a hard
turn. Brandon thrusts the note into his pocket, grabs the
wheel, wrenches it around, gets the cruiser going on course
again. Betty leans in a corner of the seat, away from him.

BETTY

Funny, I never thought of you that way. You were
so close, too. We were all pretty stupid about you.

BRANDON
(tightly)

Including Killaine.

BETTY
(softly)

Including Killaine . . . I still can't think of you
that way.

BRANDON
(staring straight ahead)

I told you my father died in jail. He stole a fortune.
Most of it's pretty dirty money. I don't care to have
that known.

148

BETTY
*(same tone)*
Larry Mitchell found out. So you killed him.

BRANDON
In a way.

BETTY
If it was an accident, you could have told the truth.

BRANDON
So could you. But our records were a little against
us.

BETTY
What your father did doesn't condemn you.

BRANDON
Nobody believed I wasn't in on it. I was just a
dumb-smart college boy, and he was my father. I
thought it was legitimate business. He was a
politician, with fingers in a lot of pies. I never saw
the pies. They had names. For the record. Innocent names.
*(he shrugs)*
You know where that kind of money comes from,
don't you?

BETTY
The money that makes you Mr. Clark Brandon.
Lets you live in a penthouse, on top of the
Vancouver Royal. Lets you own this cruiser. Lets
you do what you please, go where you please. You
big, open-handed, generous guy. That's the kind of
money it takes, isn't it?

The PLANE NOISE is a little louder. Brandon looks up at it
without much interest, then looks at Betty.

BRANDON
It buys things, just like any other kind.

149

BETTY

That man that was following us last night—he
didn't come back this morning. I'm beginning to
wonder about him, too. Was he really following
me—or you?

BRANDON

No. I paid him off.

BETTY

He'll come back . . . They always come back
when you give them money.

BRANDON

Not this one. And not Mitchell.

BETTY
(recoiling)

You—killed—him?

BRANDON
(with a twisted smile)

Magruder obliged me. No use my saying it wasn't
planned that way. I had to clean up. I'm not a
dumb-smart college boy anymore.
(he takes a deep breath)
Nobody in the world would believe I didn't plan
the whole thing.

BETTY

I guess I'm a little screwy. Maybe I could believe it.
Should I try?

BRANDON

Don't go soft on me, baby. I've got your note in my
pocket. *You* wrote it, all by your own self. And I
have to use it. It has to be found in exactly the right
place.

BETTY

So that *I* will never be found.

Brandon turns his head and stares full at her. He swallows.
He can't speak.

WIPE TO

137 INTERIOR OF PROJECTION ROOM I-BUREAU—DARK
EXCEPT FOR A STRONG WHITE LIGHT OVER A DESK

In the background there is a projection screen and a comparison projector. The police technician is bending over the desk,
looking at something through a magnifying glass, as Killaine
enters.

KILLAINE
Got anything on the Goble case yet?

The technician puts down a magnifying glass.

TECHNICIAN
Yes. I think so. Here are two glazed manila
envelopes.
*(he holds them up)*
One is the bag type. This other one had money in
it. Don't ask me how I know. I know.

KILLAINE
I'm interested in who handled it.

TECHNICIAN
Four different people, Inspector. Three men and a
woman. I've made slides for two. They handled
both envelopes.

He fits two slides into the projector and switches on the light.
Focuses a couple of separate images on the screen. One is a
complete fingerprint, the other a portion such as would be
made by a tip of a finger.

TECHNICIAN
Goble. Second finger of left hand. On the left, the
morgue print. On the right, print lifted from the
envelope.

He turns another knob and the two images draw together,
overlap, and then coincide, so that the incomplete image
disappears altogether.

151

TECHNICIAN

No doubt about that one.

KILLAINE

How about Magruder?

TECHNICIAN

He checks too.

KILLAINE

That leaves two strangers.

TECHNICIAN

So far.

KILLAINE

Try Betty Mayfield. The Mitchell case.

TECHNICIAN
(surprised)
Mayfield? She fit into this?

KILLAINE
(deadpan)
She might.

Technician opens a file drawer and takes out a fingerprint card. Lays it on the desk and picks up the magnifying glass.

TECHNICIAN

You'll have to take my word for it. We don't make slides until we have perfect prints for comparison.

KILLAINE

I'll take your word.

The technician places another card beside the one he took from the drawer, bends over, examines them through the magnifying glass, straightens up and shakes his head.

TECHNICIAN

Not a chance. Whorl and plain arch. Different as salt and sand.

152

Killaine puts his hand in his pocket and takes out another fingerprint card.

                    KILLAINE
          Try this for the second stranger.

Technician takes the card, looks at it, pushes the other cards to one side.

                    TECHNICIAN
          Gun permit, eh?
                    (he lines up two cards, studies them)
          Another whorl—man-size.

He studies the prints a moment longer, then faces Killaine.

                    TECHNICIAN
          This gun permit was issued to Clark Brandon?

                    KILLAINE
          The card says so, doesn't it?

                    TECHNICIAN
          Brandon handled the money envelope.

Killaine turns instantly, and starts out, CAMERA FOLLOW-ING. As he opens the door, he meets Driscoll coming in. Driscoll backs away, Killaine exits.

138     EXTERIOR—CORRIDOR—OUTSIDE I-BUREAU

                    KILLAINE
          What's the long face for, Driscoll?

                    DRISCOLL
          Magruder's conked out. Adrenalin injections, oxy-
          gen tent. He may come out of it and he may not.
          As a source of quick information, we can forget
          him.

                    KILLAINE
          We don't need him.

He opens door of I-Bureau.

KILLAINE

Go on in. See what they've got. All I need now is a warrant and some wings.

He goes out of SHOT quickly. Driscoll looks after him, then starts into I-Bureau.

DISSOLVE TO

139   EXTERIOR—COAST GUARD STATION—STEVESTON, BRITISH COLUMBIA

(*NOTE:* I don't know if there is a Coast Guard Station here, so just use this name at random)

There is an armed guard at the entrance and a Canadian Coast Guard flag flies over the building. A Vancouver police car drives up at high speed and squeals to a stop beside the sentry. (*NOTE:* This is a Canadian sentry, so watch what he does. I do not believe he acts the way an American sentry does, that is throwing his rifle across his body.)
Killaine leans out of the window, shows the sentry his badge.

KILLAINE

Inspector Killaine. Vancouver City Police. Commander Goodwin's expecting me.

SENTRY

Very good, sir.

He steps back. The police car speeds on.

WIPE TO

140   INTERIOR—COAST GUARD CONTROL ROOM

Radio operator at set.

RADIO OPERATOR
(*into mike*)
C.G.L. to all cutters and patrol planes on station. Vancouver Police Department bulletin. Wanted for murder. Clark Brandon. A naturalized Canadian citizen. Age 34-35. Height six feet, one inch. Weight 190 pounds. Muscular build. Dark hair. American accent. Now probably at sea in cabin

154

cruiser Valkyrie. Will probably attempt to cross International line under cover of darkness.

WIPE TO

141    MEDIUM SHOT—COAST GUARD CUTTER LYNX AT BERTH

Engines idling. A rating stands by to cast off. Killaine and a Coast Guard officer come rapidly down ramp, jump on board. Rating casts off. Lynx, a converted P.T. boat, without torpedo tubes, moves off from berth, picking up speed rapidly.

142    MEDIUM LONG SHOT—VALKYRIE TRAVELING AT HIGH SPEED IN OPEN WATER (FILTER SHOT—BETWEEN LIGHT AND DARKNESS)

PLANE NOISE high overhead.

143    INTERIOR COCKPIT OF VALKYRIE

Brandon at wheel. Betty pressed into corner of the seat watching him. Spray drifts over them.

144    MEDIUM SHOT—COAST GUARD PLANE IN FLIGHT

A converted Hudson bomber.

145    CLOSER SHOT OF PLANE

The pilot and co-pilot can be seen through the plexiglass. They are searching the water below with their eyes.

146    INTERIOR OF PLANE—SHOOTING PAST PILOT AND CO-PILOT

Pilot pushes the wheel forward and the plane goes into a steep dive.

147    REVERSE SHOT FROM PILOT'S ANGLE

The cabin cruiser is seen far below, moving fast through the water. Or rather its wake is seen. The cruiser itself, at this height, is almost invisible.

148    INTERIOR. CRUISER VALKYRIE—COCKPIT

Betty is looking up at the plane. Brandon reaches inside his coat. His hand comes out with a heavy automatic, which we have seen before.

155

BRANDON
(tightly)
Get down in the cabin, Betty.

Her eyes go down. She sees the gun, reacts. A bitter smile moves her lips.

BETTY
Why? To live ten minutes longer? And in the meantime, protect you?
(her voice becomes taunting)
Why don't you shoot me now and get it over with—
(she looks up towards the PLANE NOISE)
If you think you have time.

149     REVERSE SHOT—FROM BEHIND BRANDON'S POSITION

A fog bank about a mile ahead.

BRANDON
(as if to himself)
Always some fog out here.

He looks up in the direction of the PLANE NOISE which is increasing.

BRANDON
There'd better be.

150     BACK TO INTERIOR OF PLANE—SHOOTING FORWARD THROUGH THE PLEXIGLASS

Head and shoulders of pilot and co-pilot. The cruiser down on the water is getting rapidly larger, but still it cannot be seen who is in the cockpit, or even how many persons. The co-pilot puts a pair of binoculars to his eyes.

151     COCKPIT OF VALKYRIE

Brandon with one hand on the wheel, the other holding the gun. He is staring up towards the plane. Betty is not in the cockpit. Brandon turns towards where she was, reacts sharply, seeing she has disappeared. An expression of frustration and despair shows on his face for a moment. The

NOISE OF THE PLANE in the power dive becomes furiously loud. Brandon's head goes around again.

152    REVERSE SHOT—THE PLANE DIVING DIRECTLY ON THE VALKYRIE

Brandon sees it. It dives down almost into the CAMERA.

153    MEDIUM LONG SHOT—FROM WATER LEVEL

The Valkyrie and the plane. At the last moment, the plane pulls out of the dive, only thirty or forty feet above the Valkyrie, and goes into a climbing bank.

154    MEDIUM LONG SHOT—VALKYRIE—SHOOTING FROM BEHIND

The fog bank dead ahead. The Coast Guard plane is climbing off to the left. The Valkyrie reaches the fog bank, plunges into it, and becomes invisible.

155    INTERIOR OF VALKYRIE COCKPIT IN FOG

Brandon is steering straight ahead. He reaches to cut off the engines. The Valkyrie slows down. Betty's head emerges from the companionway. Her eyes meet Brandon's. Brandon is silent.

BETTY
You hoped I'd jumped overboard, didn't you?

Brandon does not answer, just stares at her.

BETTY
But I wouldn't make it that easy for you.

156    LONG SHOT OF COAST GUARD CUTTER LYNX TRAVEL-ING AT HIGH SPEED

157    CLOSE SHOT—BRIDGE OF LYNX

Coast Guard Lt. in command, Killaine beside him, a talker with a head set standing nearby. He is receiving a message.

TALKER
(into his mouthpiece)
Bearing one-three-five.
(to Coast Guard officer)
Bearing one-three-five, sir.

157

Coast Guard officer nods.

> COAST GUARD OFFICER
> *(to helmsman)*

Get it?

> HELMSMAN

One-three-five, sir.

He turns his wheel a little. The Lynx changes course, heeling over. Coast Guard officer puts binoculars to his eyes, swings them in a slow arc. They come to a stop, fixed.

> COAST GUARD OFFICER
> *(pointing)*

There.

Killaine follows his pointing finger.

158     WHAT THEY SEE—LONG SHOT ACROSS OPEN EMPTY WATER—A FLARE HANGING IN THE SKY AND FALLING

As it falls, it is swallowed in a bank of fog.

159     BRIDGE OF CUTTER LYNX

> KILLAINE
> *(tensely)*

Fog.

> COAST GUARD OFFICER

We got a lot of it out here.

> KILLAINE

Brandon will have counted on that.

> COAST GUARD OFFICER

No doubt. We have something he may not have counted on.

CUT TO

160     CLOSE SHOT OF VALKYRIE STOPPED IN FOG

NOISE OF THE PLANE overhead, loud but diminishing. Brandon sits listening, his hand on the wheel.

> BETTY
> *(contempt in her voice now)*
> You'll never make it. You've out-smarted yourself.

> BRANDON
> *(quietly)*
> I'm still on course to Victoria. Nobody saw you get on board, nobody's seen you since.

The Valkyrie has now stopped on the swell. It rocks a little. There are confused NOISES in the distance. PLANE NOISE, possibly some other kind of ENGINE NOISE. In the fog you can't tell what it is.

> BETTY
> You didn't leave the note.

Brandon puts the gun down close to his body, and pats his pocket.

> BRANDON
> It wasn't the time or place. Don't worry about the note, baby. I'm playing for my neck now.

> BETTY
> And I'm begging for my life—and for yours.

> BRANDON
> *(startled)*
> Mine?

> BETTY
> Yes. Yours. You haven't murdered anybody. You killed Mitchell. Wasn't that an accident? It must have been. If you kill a blackmailer, you kill him dead—so that he can't talk anymore.

> BRANDON
> Mitchell was dead enough.

BETTY

And that nasty man that followed us last night.
You didn't kill him.

BRANDON

Who'd believe it but you? I took him out to sea and
threw him in the water. Even if they find him,
what connects him with me?

BETTY

Magruder does.

BRANDON

You think Magruder wants to hang beside me?

BETTY

But the next one *is* murder. First the little step,
then the longer step, and then the step you can
never take back. You could tell about Mitchell. You
could tell about Magruder—and the detective. It
would hurt, but you could do it. You could never
tell about me.

BRANDON

Would I want to?

BETTY

Every day of your life you'll want to. You'll never
get over it. Every time you see your face in the
mirror—

BRANDON
*(with a sudden burst of fury)*
Shut up! Cut it out, I tell you! Even if I have to kill
both of us—

He breaks off with a disgusted gesture. A faint smile shows
on Betty's lips.

CUT TO

161    BRIDGE OF THE CUTTER LYNX

Killaine and the Coast Guard officer are peering ahead into
the thick fog. The Lynx is just drifting. The helmsman is

160

standing with one hand on the wheel. The Coast Guard officer turns to talker.

> COAST GUARD OFFICER
> Nothing yet?

Talker shakes his head, then:

> TALKER
> *(suddenly)*
> Just a minute, sir. I believe—

162     RADAR SCREEN BELOW THE BRIDGE

A blob of light takes form in one corner of it. CAMERA PULLS BACK TO INCLUDE THE OPERATOR. He reaches for a mike.

> OPERATOR
> *(into mike)*
> Change course about five degrees south.

After a moment the blob of light on the radar screen moves across towards the center of the screen.

> OPERATOR
> *(into mike)*
> You're dead on now. Hold it there.

163     BRIDGE OF LYNX

The four men on it are now tensely staring straight ahead.

164     CABIN CRUISER COCKPIT

Brandon is listening intently again. Far away there is a faint SOUND OF DIESEL ENGINES, but growing rapidly louder. He stands up and twists his body, still holding the gun, looks back, then slips quickly behind the wheel again.

> BRANDON
> Radar.

He guns the motor and the cabin cruiser shoots forward into high speed. Betty has to hang on. He swings the cruiser around on another course and guns it for all it is worth for a moment or two, then abruptly cuts the motors again. Cruiser slows down, once more drifts. The ENGINE SOUND has now stopped. Brandon turns to face Betty, who is now standing up.

> BRANDON
>
> This is it, Betty. They'll find us again, fog or no fog.

> BETTY
> *(speaking slowly, with difficulty)*
> If it has to be—do you mind if I do it myself?
> *(pause, then quickly)*
> Oh, I don't mean with the gun. This is no trick. When I wrote that note you have in your pocket— that was no trick either. It's not so hard for me as you think. I'm not crying about it. I've been skating close to it for quite some time. The water is cold down there—
> *(she gives a little shrug)*
> But so is everything else. And there's you.

> BRANDON
> *(startled)*
> Me?

> BETTY
> Yes. You. You're not really a murderer yet.

165     QUICK SHOT OF RADAR SCREEN

A blob of light slides into it from the other corner.

QUICK CUT TO

166     BRIDGE OF LYNX

> TALKER
> *(into his mouthpiece)*
> Bearing one-eight-one
> *(to Coast Guard officer)*
> One-eight-one, sir. Changed course due South.

> OFFICER
> *(to helmsman)*
> One-eight-one.

162

HELMSMAN
One-eight-one, sir.

Helmsman swings the wheel around. The Lynx veers, heeling over, comes level again.

167    OVERHEAD SHOT DOWN ON LYNX (FROM HELI-
       COPTER)

Following at an equal speed, then the Lynx gradually pulls away into the fog and disappears. The NOISE OF ITS ENGINES is still heard for a few moments.

168    CABIN CRUISER COCKPIT

Still motionless on the water, the motor idling. There is a SOUND OF THE CUTTER'S MOTORS, far off, but increasing. Brandon is paying no attention. He is staring at Betty.

BRANDON
(thickly)
I'm not a murderer yet, you said. Come here. Come close. Let me look at you.

Betty holds off, then slowly comes towards him along the seat, until their faces are close. He searches her eyes.

BRANDON
(quietly)
I think you mean that.

BETTY
Did you think I was faking?

BRANDON
(thickly)
If I did—I don't—now.

He puts his arms around her, pulls her close. There is a kind of wonder in his eyes. Hers stare back at him, calm and level. He kisses her hard on the mouth, lets her go. She pulls away from him, along the seat. She doesn't know what to think of him. She is terrified, resigned, and at the same time, he still has an attraction for her.

163

> BRANDON

The kiss of death.

> (laughs)

With a new twist.

He lifts the gun in his hand, looks at it, tosses it overboard. He reaches inside his coat, takes out the suicide note.

> BRANDON
> (reading)

"Dear Inspector Killaine. This is goodbye. You were right. I had a secret."

The DIESEL ENGINE SOUND has grown louder. Brandon looks up from the note.

> BRANDON

A secret, Betty—as who hasn't?

He crumples the note and envelope in his hand, drops them over the side of the boat. Opens the engine full throttle and the power of the cruiser almost tears it out from under them. Betty is thrown violently against the seat. He reaches out and straightens her up. There is a mad light in his eyes now. His face is no longer hard.

169
to
172
SERIES OF HELICOPTER SHOTS of the chase, alternating with the cabin cruiser and the Lynx, as the Lynx gradually closes in. During these shots the cabin cruiser and the Lynx both come out of the fog bank into moonlit water, but there is another fog bank half a mile or so ahead.

173
INTERIOR OF VALKYRIE COCKPIT—SHOOTING BACK

The Lynx is moving up fast, and the Coast Guard officer can be seen on the bridge, with binoculars to his eyes. A rating, hanging on tight, is stripping the canvas off a twin machine gun mount.

> BRANDON
> (above the roar of the motors)

Stand up! Let them take a good look at you. Be sure they see you. That fellow back there has night glasses. Then jump—well out to the side. Just as far out as you can.

Betty does what he tells her. She waves. There is an answering wave from the bridge of the Lynx. We can't see who it is waving. Betty sets herself to jump. She tries to speak to Brandon, but nothing comes out. There is a great deal of NOISE from motors. Gravely Brandon lifts his hand and salutes her. She jumps.

174 FOLLOWING SHOT AS BETTY HITS THE WATER AND THE CRUISER PULLS AWAY RAPIDLY

towards another fog bank beyond the clear space.

QUICK CUT TO

175 BRIDGE OF LYNX

                    COAST GUARD OFFICER
Full speed astern.

                    TALKER
Full speed astern.

The cutter heaves on reversed engines, nearly stands on its tail in the water, drifts past Betty, comes to a stop, then moves forward slowly, swinging around to get close to her.

176 HIGH FOLLOWING SHOT CABIN CRUISER

As it reaches the fog and plunges into it. HELICOPTER WITH CAMERA plunges into fog at same time.

177 CLOSE SHOT—CUTTER LYNX

Stopped on the swell. Betty in the water, fighting her way towards it. A life belt and rope are dropped neatly beside her. She grasps it and is drawn towards the side of the Lynx. Coast Guard officer, Killaine, and a rating put rope ladder over the side. Killaine starts down rope ladder.

178 REVERSE SHOT—DOWN FROM DECK OF LYNX

Past Killaine on rope ladder to water, as Betty is pulled to foot of ladder. Killaine reaches down, gets her hand. She grasps rope ladder, Killaine helps her up onto it. Business of getting her on board cutter.

179    INTERIOR—VALKYRIE COCKPIT

Brandon, staring straight ahead of him, gripping the wheel hard, giving the cruiser everything it has, driving as if he had a clear, open course. HEARS A FOGHORN, somewhere off in the fog. Cocks his head, tries to gauge the direction. Turns the wheel a little.

180    DECK OF LYNX

As Betty comes over the side, Killaine holding her up. Betty is shivering with cold. The rating hauls up the rope ladder and the life belt. Coast Guard officer signals the bridge and the Lynx starts moving ahead again.

> COAST GUARD OFFICER
> *(to Betty)*
> Better get those wet clothes off in a hurry, Miss. My cabin's at your disposal.

> BETTY
> Thank you. Thank you very much.

He salutes, turns away, after giving a quick look at Killaine.

> BETTY
> *(to Killaine)*
> He could have killed me a dozen times. You'd never have known.

> KILLAINE
> We know everything

> BETTY
> *(almost passionately)*
> No, Jeff. You don't. He's not a murderer, I tell you. He's not a murderer.

> KILLAINE
> *(same tone)*
> I hope he can prove it. Come on. You don't want to get pneumonia.

He takes her arm, starts to push her along. She is still shivering, but still determined to defend Brandon.

BETTY
But I tell you—if you'd only understand.

KILLAINE
(gently)
I understand, Betty. I understand perfectly.

He puts his arm around her. Their eyes meet in a long look.

181 INTERIOR OF VALKYRIE COCKPIT

The cruiser is moving at high speed in the fog. The FOG-HORN SOUND is louder, but seems to come from all directions. Brandon is leaning forward, tensely, trying to see ahead. He turns the wheel first one way, and then another. There is a sudden blast of the FOGHORN, very loud.

Brandon turns the wheel violently and the cruiser keels over. But he is not quick enough. Suddenly above looms the enormous bow of the Puget Sound ferry, as big as an ocean liner. It is ablaze with light. CAMERA PANS UP to show it crashing right down into the lens, as it were.

182 THE CRUISER

Thrown out of the water almost, it is up-ended on its stern. The ferry tears on through, filling the screen.

QUICK CUT TO

183 A CORNER OF THE PASSENGER DECK OF THE FERRY

A couple of passengers in overcoats leaning against the rail, looking out into the fog. One of them is lighting a cigarette, cupping his hands around the lighter.

FIRST PASSENGER
You always have this kind of weather up here?

SECOND PASSENGER
Certain times of the year. Always a lot of fog. But they never hit anything, somehow.

QUICK CUT TO

184 BRIDGE OF THE FERRY

At the end of the bridge an officer is leaning down, staring towards the water. He shakes his head, straightens up, turns away.

OFFICER
*(speaking off)*
An old packing case, I guess.

185     A BIG SEARCHLIGHT

Its beam is turned down on the water. The beam moves a little, back towards the stern. CAMERA FOLLOWS THE BEAM DOWN THROUGH THE FOG. Empty water, only, is seen. The searchlight is switched off.

WIPE TO

186     DARK FOGGY SHOT—CLOSE TO SURFACE OF WATER

A broken piece of the cabin cruiser's bow floats by, closer and closer to the camera, until on it the name VALKYRIE stands out, then it whirls past. There is nothing left but the foggy surface of the Sound.